Reading the Old Testament
Through Jewish Eyes

READING THE OLD TESTAMENT THROUGH JEWISH EYES

Book
978-1-7910-0624-2 *Paperback*
978-1-7910-0625-9 *ePub*

Leader Guide
978-1-7910-0626-6 *Paperback*
978-1-7910-0627-3 *ePub*

DVD
978-1-7910-0628-0

ALSO BY RABBI EVAN MOFFIC

*What Every Christian Needs
to Know About Judaism*

*What Every Christian Needs
to Know About Passover*

*What Every Christian Needs
to Know About the Jewishness of Jesus*

First the Jews

Shalom for the Heart

READING THE OLD TESTAMENT THROUGH JEWISH EYES

RABBI EVAN MOFFIC

Abingdon Press | Nashville

READING THE OLD TESTAMENT
THROUGH JEWISH EYES

Library of Congress Control Number: 2021939039
ISBN 13: 978-1-7910-0624-2

Unless otherwise noted, Scripture translations are taken from TANAKH: The New JPS Translation According to the Traditional Hebrew Text. Copyright 1985 by the Jewish Publication Society. Used by permission.

Scripture quotations noted CEB are taken from the Common English Bible, copyright 2011. Used by permission. All rights reserved.

21 22 23 24 25 26 27 28 29 30—10 9 8 7 6 5 4 3 2 1
MANUFACTURED IN THE UNITED STATES OF AMERICA

CONTENTS

CONTENTS

CHAPTER 1

THE TORAH

Two years ago I received an unexpected invitation. The president of a prominent Christian seminary told me they had received a Torah scroll as a donation. They planned a ceremony to dedicate it. Would I be willing to deliver a prayer at the ceremony?

I was intrigued. Torah scrolls are usually found only in synagogues or museums. I wondered what the seminary planned to do with the scroll. Was it something they would simply display in the library or a museum? Or did they intend to study and learn from it?

I soon learned the answer. The gift of the scroll was part of a larger project to aid Christians in the study of the Torah. A philanthropist from Minnesota had donated over thirty scrolls to seminaries around the world.

During the dedication ceremony, one of the seminary's professors remarked that "Our roots are much deeper and wider than we thought. Jesus celebrated the festivals. Jesus taught the verses of the Torah. When I

1

grasped that and read the Torah, it all came to life in a whole new way."

The ceremony included a reading from the Torah and a discussion of its message. I was the concluding speaker, with two minutes to say a prayer. The prayer I wrote brought the assembly back to the creation of that particular scroll, which happened in a small town in Poland in the 1700s. The man who wrote it, I said, would never have imagined that the words he slowly inked onto the parchment would be studied three hundred years later—in Chicago, Illinois—by Christian seminary students.

It was, I said, another reminder of what we all know. God's power and vision are greater and wider than we can ever imagine.

This book began that day. Before that experience, I saw Torah as synonymous with Jews and Judaism. This view seemed to make sense. The great teachers of Torah wrote and spoke primarily in Hebrew. Jewish worship centers around the reading and study of the Torah. And over much of its history, Christianity for its part saw the Torah as simply the precursor to the New Testament. Its teachings, many Christians believed, fit better in a museum than a seminary.

But this view no longer makes sense. Hundreds of thousands of Christians have visited Israel and seen the place where Torah lived and from where Jesus emerged. They have experienced the sights, sounds, and places described in Torah and realize the view of life taught in Torah permeated Jesus's teachings.

As I saw in the seminary that day, we also live in a time of yearning for a deeper and wider faith. The wisdom and practices of Torah draw us closer together and closer to the one God of us all. Indeed, putting Torah in the hands of all people was God's purpose all along. The Torah itself makes clear that it is not meant for Jews only. God's words speak to everyone. In a beautiful passage in Deuteronomy, God says to Moses,

> *Surely, this Instruction which I enjoin upon you this day is not too baffling for you, nor is it beyond reach. It is not in the heavens, that you should say, "Who among us can go up to the heavens and get it for us and impart it to us, that we may observe it?" Neither is it beyond the sea, that you should say, "Who among us can cross to the other side of the sea and get it for us and impart it to us, that we may observe it?" No, the thing is very close to you, in your mouth and in your heart, to observe it*
>
> Deuteronomy 30:11-14

The Torah's message waits for us in its scrolls.

This book invites you into the world of Torah. It is not the Torah of endless laws and rituals. It is the Torah of truth, wisdom, and transformation. It is the Torah received by Moses, studied by Jesus, and carried in the arms of the Jewish people to this day. As you read this book, *the Torah* will become *your Torah*. You will see your life, struggles, questions, and history captured in its stories and characters. You will drink more deeply from the rich reservoir from which billions of people have found the deepest truths and insights about God and life. This book will be your guide in taking the Torah out of the ark where it is kept and bringing it into your life.

As we take hold of Torah, we will also be guided by some of its greatest teachers from the last two thousand years. The teachings of these sages help us see the depth and breadth of God's word. These teachers are like a wise friend who sits next to us at a concert. They know the music backward and forward. They have spent their life studying it. They notice things we do not notice and give us information about the author, composer, melodies, notes, and tempo we would never know. Some of these teachers may even have been alive with Jesus. They knew him, studied with him. God's word was like the air they breathed. They help us appreciate and live it. You will hear their words throughout this book.

WHAT IS TORAH?

The word *Torah* means "teaching" or "process." The phrase "*the Torah*" refers to the first five books of the Bible. This distinction is important. Sometimes Jews use the phrase word "Torah" by itself to refer to all Jewish sacred texts. For example, someone could say "I'm studying Torah this afternoon," but he or she could mean the study of rabbinic writings or prayers.

But if someone says I'm studying "the Torah" this afternoon, they are referring to the five books of Moses.

This book is about *the Torah, which* consists of the books of Genesis, Exodus, Leviticus, Numbers, and Deuteronomy—the first five books of the Bible for both Jews and Christians. In addition to its division into five books, the Torah is also divided into fifty-four sections known in Hebrew as *parashiyot*, which means "Torah portions." Jews read one Torah portion in the synagogue every week, with occasional changes because of holidays. Most synagogues read through the entire Torah over the course of one year.

Reading the Torah is a sacred responsibility. Sometimes the rabbi will read from the Torah. Sometimes it is a devout member of the community. Sometimes a young man or woman who is undergoing a rite of passage called a bar or bat mitzvah will read from the Torah. This responsibility demands preparation because the reader does not simply read the English translation of the Torah portion from a book. He or she will usually chant the Hebrew text in a melody developed thousands of years ago. This melody is called *nusach*, and it developed in ancient Persia and Babylonia as a way of remembering the words of the Torah text. Few Torah scrolls existed at the time, so scribes and other religious scholars would memorize the text according to a melody, and then chant from the text every week. That melody carries on today when we read every week from the Torah. This connection with history is part of what makes Torah sacred and meaningful. It is the word of God cherished, sung, and celebrated by Jews for over two thousand years.

LETTERS IN THE TORAH

The Torah is not only chanted in an ancient, particular way. It is also written in a sacred style that is twenty-five hundred years old. Every Torah scroll is handwritten by a scribe or team of scribes. They spend between twelve and eighteen months writing it. The Hebrew word for scribe is *sofer*. The same Hebrew word also means "count." The scribe traditionally counts all the letters of Torah as he or she writes them.

Why do such details matter? Because every part of God's word contains truth and meaning. If we miss a letter or detail, our perspective is incomplete. Our view of God's word is potentially distorted. The importance of getting every letter of Torah properly written is the basis for beautiful teachings about the importance of every human being. One eighteenth-century rabbi said that every human being is like a letter in the Torah scroll. If one is missing, the story is incomplete. Every human being is part of God's story, and our birth and entry into the world is part of God's story.

The scribe also uses a special ink mixture made from a two-thousand-year-old recipe found in the Talmud. That recipe involved boiling oils, tar, and wax, and collecting the vapors. Then the scribe would add tree sap and honey, let it dry, and store it. According to a leading modern scribe, "The ink needs to be durable, but not indelible.... Today, most [scribes] make ink by boiling crushed gallnuts together with gum arabic and copper sulfate. Carbon is also added at times, allowing the ink to dry to a deep shiny black. The shiny black ink on the white parchment alludes to the Torah being given as 'black fire on white fire.'"[1]

A special quill is used for writing. It is usually made from a turkey feather. The scribe typically uses a different special quill when writing the name of God. The parchment must be from the skin of a kosher animal, often a lamb or a goat. The parchments are sewn together and wrapped around wooden rollers. No metal is used in the creation of a Torah scroll, because metal is used to make instruments of war, whereas the Torah's ultimate value is shalom, *peace*. In addition, no tree may be cut down to make wood for the Torah rollers. The tree must have died naturally. Scribes devote years to studying the practice of writing a scroll.

Handling a Torah scroll also requires careful attention. We avoid placing our hands or fingers directly on the parchment because the oils and bacteria from our hands can erode it. When reading from the scroll, the Torah reader typically uses a pointer called a *yad*, which means "hand" in Hebrew. Artists have created *yads* reflecting the style and values of their communities. My first confirmation class at the synagogue where I taught when I was a student gave me a *yad* to celebrate my ordination as a rabbi. Every time I read from the Torah, I am reminded of my sacred responsibility to live and share its truths.

The construction and method for reading from the Torah are so precise because, as it is often pointed out about many topics, God is in the details. Our human actions serve a divine purpose. Indeed, we enact God's will and observe Torah values in the very way we construct a Torah. Using a special quill for God, for example, illustrates the sanctity we attach to the divine name. Writing that name requires special focus and intention. Not using base metals reminds us of the ultimate purpose of a life of Torah: bringing about a world of peace. Even the process of disposing of a Torah reflects Torah values. When a Torah scroll is no longer usable—this status usually results from wear and tear or damage—it is buried. A Torah scroll can never be destroyed. We lovingly say goodbye and bury a Torah scroll as a sign of our sacred relationship to its words and Author.

This respect given to God's word exerts so much influence on Jewish life that it has inspired people of other faiths. Consider what happened at a New Orleans synagogue, 114 years old, named Congregation Beth Israel. In 2005, in the wake of Hurricane Katrina, the rabbis and members of the congregation had no access to their building. It was four blocks from the biggest water canal breach in the city. The synagogue was flooded with eight feet of water. They had left their seven Torah scrolls, most of which were over 100 years old, in the sanctuary ark before the storm because they figured it would pass over in two or three days. When the storm did not relent and the synagogue members scattered around the country, they concluded the Torah scrolls were ruined. But two weeks after the storm, they learned that the scrolls had been rescued. The scrolls, however, had largely melted and "disintegrated into formless goo."[2] The man who rescued them wanted to take them to a synagogue in Baton Rouge, but the leaders of the Temple Beth Israel believed they needed to be buried immediately near their previous home. They put out a call for help in burying the scrolls, and a Christian woman who lived nearby—and who had worked at the synagogue for 8 years—volunteered. She retrieved them, cleaned and preserved all the crowns and yads, placed what remained of the scrolls in a vinyl tablecloth so that they would not touch the ground, dug a six-by-six hole in her backyard, and placed the scrolls in it. In its death, as in life, a Torah scroll promotes the best within us.

When the Torah is not being read, it typically rests in a receptacle in the synagogue known as an ark. The ark is enclosed in or connected to the eastern wall of the sanctuary of the synagogue, as a way of pointing toward Jerusalem. The ark holding the scrolls echoes the portable ark carried through the Sinai desert on the journey from Egypt to the land of Israel. It is considered the most sacred place in the synagogue. The various Hebrew names for the ark illustrate this belief. One way of referring to the ark is the *aron hakodesh*, which means "the holy ark." The word *kadosh* means both "holy" and "set apart," indicating the ark's sacred status. Other Jewish texts refer to the ark as the *teva*, which is the same Hebrew used to refer to Noah's ark in the Bible. Like Noah's ark, the words of Torah are the *teva* sustaining human life. The final name used is *heikhal*, which means "palace." In the Jerusalem Temple, the first of which stood from about 940 to 586 BCE, and the second of which from 531 BCE to 70 CE, the *heikhal* was the inner sanctum of the sanctuary where the menorah, altar of incense, and table of the showbread stood.

The ark of contemporary synagogues echoes this inner sanctum of the Jerusalem Temple. The belief behind this linguistic and architectural connection is that when the Temple stood, God lived in the Temple. When the Temple was destroyed, God's presence went with the Jewish people wherever they set up communities. The Torah scroll is evidence of God within the midst of the Jewish people. Thus, the Torah scroll rests in the *heikhal*, a symbol of the place where God once resided. As one poet put it, the Torah is the "portable homeland of the Jewish people." Some Holocaust survivors had scraps of Torah scrolls with them. They brought it with them as a source of comfort, strength, and hope.

This belief illustrates another critical role Torah plays for the Jewish community. The Torah represents God on earth. God is found not in the parchment or the ink. God rests in the words and letters we read. In Christianity, God became flesh. In Judaism, God becomes Torah. Now, the Torah itself is not a living, breathing entity, but its words make God present. This truth is one of the reasons a Torah reader has to prepare so extensively. Making a mistake distorts God's name itself. That's why another sacred task is the *gabbai*, who stands next to the Torah reader and follows along as he or she is reading and corrects any mistakes made. Of course, readers make mistakes, but the gabbai is there to make an immediate correction so that worshippers are not misled. This act of correcting is not intended to shame or embarrass the reader. It is considered an act of kindness because everyone in the sanctuary wants to hear the text accurately.

This focus on a perfect reading may seem strange and perhaps overly legalistic. Doesn't the spirit of the reader count more than the precise accuracy of what they are reading? Yes, it does, and that's why the Jewish sages made a distinction between major mistakes and minor mistakes. A minor mistake is a mispronunciation of a word. This happens easily because the Torah text in a scroll does not contain vowels. The vowels—known in Hebrew as *nikudot*—are included only in printed versions of the Torah, not the Torah scrolls written by scribes. The Torah reader studies those printed versions before reading publicly from the scroll. Still, using the wrong voweling while reading from the scroll happens easily and frequently. In these cases, If the Torah reader makes a pronunciation error and it does not confuse the meaning of the word, it is considered a minor mistake. Minor mistakes also include placing emphasis on the wrong syllable in a word, or temporarily losing the proper melody for chanting.

A major mistake—one that requires correction—is one that changes the meaning of a word. Even in these cases, however, Jewish law allows for an exception. The exception is that if correcting the mistake might embarrass the Torah reader, the gabbai should refrain from doing so. Embarrassing someone in public is a grievous sin in Jewish law. Some rabbis compare it to murder, arguing the reddening of a face when someone feels shame is like the spilling of blood. This focus on the feelings of the Torah reader illustrates the underlying purpose of Torah. It is not a rote legal requirement. It is a sacred act meant to ennoble, inspire, and guide human beings. Any practice around the reading of the Torah that detracts from these values—even if it is done out of respect for God's word—is not permitted.

HOW TORAH IS READ

The Torah reading does not include just the reader and the gabbai. It involves other participants, including those who are listening to the chanting. The involvement of the entire community in the reading of the Torah echoes the original reading and revelation of the Torah by Moses to the Israelites at Mount Sinai. The weekly reading of the Torah on the Sabbath in the synagogue reenacts this sacred moment. We are to experience the words of Torah just as the ancient Israelites did in the wilderness.

Aside from the Torah reader (known in Hebrew as the *baal korei*) and the *gabbai*, the other main participants are the those who are called to say a blessing over the Torah known as an *aliyah*. The word *aliyah* means "ascent." We ascend to a new spiritual plane when we bless the Torah. This belief explains why the Torah is often read from an elevated area of the sanctuary. It is both a physical and a spiritual ascent.

The word *aliyah*, is also used to refer to immigrating to Israel. Again, moving to the Holy Land is both a physical and a spiritual ascent. Physically, we are closer to the sacred space of the Jerusalem Temple. Spiritually, we are closer to God.

Referring to the blessing over the Torah as an aliyah reflects the role the Torah came to play in Jewish life after Jews were exiled from Israel by the Romans in 70 CE. At that time, as the poet Heinrich Heine pointed out, the Torah became the Jews' "portable homeland." Whenever a person came to bless the Torah, they ascended into the Holy Land.

The aliyah blessing begins the way every standard Jewish blessing begins: "Blessed are You, Eternal God, Sovereign of the Universe, Who commands us to..." The phrase after "to" is what makes the blessing unique. It refers to God as the One who "chose us from all the peoples of the earth and gave us the Torah." In other words, we are thanking God for giving us the gift of the Torah. I see this blessing as a reminder not to take the Torah for granted. We did not write it. We did not even deserve it. Rather, God gave it to us as a gift. It is an act of grace. It is unmerited, and it illustrates God's love.

Some Jewish theologians criticize the idea of Jews as God's chosen people as stated in this blessing. They say it smacks of ethnic chauvinism and a feeling of superiority. It is as if, they argue, Jews are saying that God chose us for the gift of Torah because we were the most worthy of all the nations of the earth. But some of the most respected rabbis in Jewish tradition argued that God made the Torah available to all peoples, and it was only Moses and the Israelites who accepted it. In any case, even if God chose to give the Torah to the Jews, God did not say that the Torah's teachings are for Jews only. As God says to Abraham in Genesis 12, "All the families of the earth Shall bless themselves by you." The Torah is the vehicle through which the Jewish people bring blessings to the world.

After the blessing, the Torah reader chants a section from the Torah. Then the same person who said the opening aliyah blessings says a closing blessing. It begins with the same words and concludes by describing God as the "One who has given us a Torah of truth and implanted eternal life within us." This blessing sees the Torah as the key means to the eternal life of the Jewish people. So long as we read and follow the words of the Torah, God will keep us alive.

A typical Torah reading contains between three and seven aliyah blessings. The person called to say an aliyah often has a connection to the Torah reader or is someone honored for a particular reason. At my synagogue, for example, when a young man or woman who is becoming a bar or bat mitzvah (a child becomes a bar or bat mitzvah through a coming-of-age ceremony that involves reading from the Torah), parents or grandparents and other relatives are invited for an aliyah. I also invite visitors to the synagogue if they are open to it, volunteers for the community, or other rabbis and community leaders. In the nineteenth century, a common practice was to offer the aliyah blessings to people who made donations to the synagogue. That practice changed because many people thought it crass, and that it undermined the purpose of the ritual, which is to elevate our moral behavior and not simply honor the wealthy. Synagogue financial practices also changed so that worshippers supported the synagogue by making annual contributions rather than a gift for a particular ritual.

HAGBA

After the final Torah reading, there is space for several communal prayers. These are prayers of both petition and gratitude, reflecting a view that the presence of Torah adds a sacred dimension to their recitation. Somehow God feels more present while the Torah is out.

After the reading of the Torah portion is complete, the Torah is lifted in a ritual called *hagba*. The person performing *hagba* takes hold of the two rollers of the Torah with each hand and gently lifts the scroll and turns around with his or her back to the congregation. The purpose is to show the community the scroll and the words of Torah written on it. Some scholars suggest the practice began twenty-five hundred years ago when community leaders feared some synagogues were reading from false or corrupt Torah scrolls. They feared the people would be confused if they heard teachings supposedly from the Torah that were not there. Therefore, they mandated that the Torah reader or another person lift the Torah scroll and show it to the community to prove to them that he or she was reading from a proper Torah scroll.

After *hagba*, another person or group of people dress the Torah in its ornamental ritual items. The first is a piece of protective fabric known as the "mantle of the law." Sometimes it is made of silk, and quite often it serves as a work of art with a quotation from the Torah on it. Then over the mantle we place the priestly breastplate. This breastplate has many potential meanings. It echoes the breastplate worn by the high priest in the Jerusalem Temple. The Book of Exodus describes it in detail. It included twelve stones representing the twelve tribes of Israel. The priestly breastplate also held two stones known as the urim and thumim. These stones were meant as a way for the high priest to discern the future. In practice, scholars believe they served as an oracle and a tool for interpreting dreams, though later books of the Bible cast doubt on their ability to predict the future. They are one of the Bible's enduring mysteries.

The use of a priestly breastplate on the Torah scroll illustrates a key reason Torah emerged as central to Judaism. When the Temple existed in Jerusalem and the Levitical priests oversaw the offerings of sacrifices as described in the Book of Leviticus, Torah's role was secondary to sacrifices. Offering an animal sacrifice was the primary way of growing closer to God. Even the Hebrew word for sacrifice—*korban*—means "closeness." Torah was part of Jewish life, and small groups of Jews led by teachers known as Pharisees would learn Torah, but priestly offerings defined proper worship.

In 70 CE, the Romans destroyed the Temple. The priestly system had no place in Jewish life. The only ongoing practice within the Jewish community was the study of Torah. The only group with the influence and organization to lead the Jewish community was the Pharisees. There were competing groups like former priests, but the Pharisees—who eventually became known as "the Rabbis"—had the political skill to negotiate with their Roman rulers and built institutions that helped sustain Judaism after the destruction of the Temple.

Torah was central to the Pharisaic worldview. They saw Torah as God's unmediated word—study of Torah and practice of Torah laws replaced sacrificial offerings. They argued that replacing sacrifices with study of Torah had been God's intent all along, as illustrated in Exodus, "you shall be to Me a kingdom of priests." Study and practice of Torah were offerings from all Israelites, not just Levitical priests. In fact, the priesthood had deterred some from closeness to God because it built up an elite class. Torah, however, was democratic and accessible to all. The rabbis implemented public education, creating a literate population of nearly 100 percent of adult males. They added two weekly Torah readings in addition to the Sabbath—Mondays and Thursdays. They chose these days because they were market days when farmers and merchants would gather in a town square or public area. The rabbis understood they needed to bring Torah to where the people were, and Torah readings became a thrice-weekly event.

They traced the importance of public reading of the Torah back to the prophet Ezra. Like the Pharisees, Ezra led the people during a time of loss and confusion. He lived the first part of his life as a Jew in Babylonia, which was then ruled by the Persians. The Persians had conquered much of the ancient Near East, including the land of Israel and Judah, which the Babylonians had controlled decades earlier. In the middle of the fifth century BCE, Ezra returned to his homeland, to Jerusalem. According to the Bible, he found the people straying from Torah. They had intermingled with other ethnic groups and, in both public and private, they were violating core laws and practices of the Torah. He feared for the survival of the Jewish people.

He sent out word that in three days, the people should gather in Jerusalem. There he read the entire Torah scroll to the people. They began observing the holidays again. They returned to following the Torah. According to the rabbinic sages, they returned to Torah with the same fervor as the generation after Moses, which was led by Joshua.

Ezra pioneered the public reading of Torah as a means of religious cohesion and renewal. In time of trouble, we turn to the Torah for guidance. This pattern has recurred throughout history. In Germany in the 1930s, as Hitler and the Nazis rose to power, synagogue attendance soared. New schools of Jewish learning began even as persecution of Jews increased. In the fifteenth and sixteenth centuries, as the massive

Jewish population of Spain was expelled and the people searched for new homes, a new school of Torah study known as Kabbalah arose. The mystical and esoteric teachers of the Kabbalah studied the Torah to find guidance, to make sense of and cope with their suffering and exile. They ultimately developed a new method of Torah study called Lurianic Kabbalah.

The foundation of this method of study is the belief that God initially created two worlds. The first was the world of *tohu v'vohu*. That is a phrase appearing in the second verse of the Book of Genesis usually translated "as empty and full of chaos." Most interpretations of the Torah picture the creation of the universe as God bringing order to this chaos. The mystics, however, interpret it as a separate world of chaos. It was the result of God's first experiment with creation. God created the first universe filled with vessels of light, but the light of God's presence was so overwhelming that the vessels shattered and the universe imploded. The mystics call this phenomenon *shevirat hakelim* (the shattering of the vessels).

In creating the next universe, God limited the divine light evident in the world so as not to overwhelm and shatter its vessels of light. This dimming of God's light helped the mystics explain why tragedies occur. Since we cannot see all of God's light, God's ways are not clear. We do not always understand why bad things happen to good people, or why God's creation unfolds the way it does. Yet, this limited perspective is not our ultimate fate. We have the ability to gather more light and make God's presence shine brighter, because the shards of light from the first universe are embedded throughout our universe. According to the mystics, when we study Torah and observe its laws, we are gathering those original sparks of light. The more sparks we gather, the closer we come to God. When all the sparks are gathered, the Messiah will arrive and the world will be redeemed.

This mystical perspective spread throughout the Jewish community in the seventeenth and eighteenth centuries. It helps us see why Torah study is so central to Jewish life. The more we study and follow it, the closer we come to redemption.

Redemption in Judaism, however, is not simply something new. While there are different perspectives on what redemption means, one prominent thread sees redemption as a return to an earlier perfection. It is a return to either the peace of the garden of Eden or the time of biblical Israel in which King David sat on the throne. This view of redemption as a return rather than something new helps us understand the last part of the Torah reading service.

Before we discuss that, however, I need to make an important point. While this mystical perspective on the importance of Torah does motivate some Jews to study, many others study Torah for different reasons. One ancient rabbi taught that the Torah has seventy faces. Each face might represent a reason we study it. For example, I teach a weekly Torah study class at my synagogue. About forty people attend regularly. While a couple of people in the class see their study as a religious obligation—one that brings us closer to God—many others simply enjoy the intellectual discussion. They like looking at the ideas and stories of the Torah. They enjoy discussing ways the truths and commandments of the Torah help us understand modern political, moral, and social challenges. Other participants study Torah because they see it as their story. It is like a family history we cherish and seek to understand. Others simply enjoy coming together as a community. Study of Torah is an excuse to gather together and share ideas. These and many other reasons help us see why Torah defines modern Jewish life.

The last part of the Torah service returns the Torah to the ark. The person who lifted the Torah—*hagba*—has usually been holding it since the conclusion of the reading. After the prayers mentioned earlier in the chapter are recited, the congregation stands and the *hagba* approaches the ark. We then recite another set of prayers accompanying the return of the Torah to the ark. These prayers consist mainly of verses from the biblical books of Psalms and Proverbs. Two verses exemplify the theme of this concluding part of the Torah reading. The first is a verse from the Book of Proverbs. We recite it as we hold the Torah, saying, "It is a tree of life to those who hold fast to it. Its ways are ways of pleasantness, and all its paths are peace."

Describing the Torah as a "tree of life" echoes the exact phrase from Genesis 2, where the "tree of life" stood in middle of the garden of Eden. The message is that if we truly lived and followed the words of Torah, we would be restored to the condition of paradise found in the garden. The Jewish sages also interpreted the verse to mean that a good life is the fruit that comes from the Torah, the tree of life. We experience pleasantness and peace when we till and tend to it.

The other verse we sing at the very end of the Torah service. It conveys a seemingly paradoxical message. We ask God to *chadesh yameinu k'kedem*, which means "to renew our days as of old." Another potential translation is "Make our days new as they were in the past." On the surface, this verse does not make sense. If something happened in the past, then it is not new. And if something is new, it did not happen in the past.

The answer to this paradox lies in the purpose of a life of Torah. When we live a life of Torah, we find new qualities of character and commitment in ourselves. Torah refines the human character. We find that we are capable and understanding of much more about our closeness to God and human experience. At the same time, we are returning to a message God revealed long ago. Torah returns us to a self that was implanted within us by God millions of years ago. This belief is captured in another Hebrew word, *teshuvah*. It is often translated into English as "repentance." But it really means "return." *Teshuvah* is a return to our highest selves. Torah is the path of that return.

OTHER PRACTICES

After we place the Torah in the ark, we carefully try not to turn our backs to the Torah. While this custom is not ordained in Jewish law, it reflects a feeling of respect toward the Torah. At my synagogue, approaching and walking away from our ark requires navigating a short set of stairs. Walking backward from the ark is tricky, but I've developed the muscle memory so that my steps feel automatic, and it demonstrates to the congregation the love and honor we give to Torah.

Some of the practices around handling and reading from the Torah differ based on the type of Jewish community. In modern Judaism, we have three primary denominations: Reform, Conservative, and Orthodox. Reform tends to balance traditional Jewish practices with modern life. Conservative Judaism, like Reform, seeks a balance between tradition and change, but it tends to err more on the side of tradition than Reform. Orthodoxy seeks to adhere as closely as possible to Jewish tradition as practiced in the sixteenth and seventeenth centuries, though even Orthodoxy has various denominations that follow different traditions.

For the purpose of understanding the role of Torah, however, the three denominations generally follow the same practice of reading through the entire scroll over one year and studying it regularly at least once a week. One key difference, however, is the way they view the authorship of the Torah. Orthodox Jews tend to see the Torah as the unmediated word of God. Its verses are open to interpretation, but they cannot be amended or seen as reflecting any human biases. The Torah is God's word given on Mount Sinai to Moses.

Reform and Conservative Jews tend to see the Torah as the work of divinely inspired human beings. These beings felt God's presence, and the stories and laws they wrote down captured the story of their people and what God commanded the Jewish people to do. They also included legends, traditions, and genealogies inherent in both their and surrounding cultures. For Reform and Conservative Jews, human authorship does not make the Torah less important. Rather, we recognize the importance of Torah comes from the meaning we assign to it. We choose, as our ancestors throughout history have chosen, to endow the words of Torah with sacred meaning. Viewing the Torah as the work of divinely inspired humans opens up the path for more comprehensive understanding as well. For example, since we recognize the words of Torah as originating in different times and places, we can examine archaeology and history to better understand the stories and ideas its authors sought to convey. Since we recognize that the human beings who wrote the Torah encountered some of the same emotional and social challenges we do today, we can examine and seek guidance in the ways they responded. The Torah has sustained the Jewish people for thousands of years because it speaks to and guides us in our deepest human needs and possibilities. This book will guide you in seeing and applying this Torah wisdom in your life.

STRUCTURE

Together, the five books of the Torah tell the story of the emergence of the Jewish people and their journey from slavery to freedom. Yet, each book also has a distinctive theme. Genesis is about family and the relationships within them. From Cain and Abel to Joseph and his brothers, Genesis reveals truths and guidance about the way we struggle to build meaningful relationships with our family. The first chapter will examine key verses from the Book of Genesis focused on this theme.

In chapter 2 we will unpack the Book of Exodus. Exodus tells the story of the emergence of the Jewish people as a nation and faith. We will examine key verses from Exodus that help us understand how we form groups and cultures in the modern world and find our place of belonging in them. In an increasingly divided world brimming with religious and ethnic conflict, returning to the Torah's wisdom can help each of us do what we can to bring about greater peace and harmony.

The Book of Leviticus challenges modern readers in its focus on the seemingly archaic details of the Jerusalem Temple. In my Torah study class, I often hear a sigh when we arrive at Leviticus. It seems thoroughly disconnected from modern life.

When read through a certain perspective, however, Leviticus may be the most practical book of the Torah. Leviticus teaches us the power of ritual. It shows the way habits and routines can influence us far more than beliefs and dogma. Leviticus also helps us understand the meaning of sacrifice. On the surface, the sacrificial offerings described in Leviticus are about what we must sacrifice for God. God requires our offering as part of sovereignty over us. When we read Leviticus closely, however, we see that it is not about sacrifices for God. It teaches us about sacrifices to God. The distinction may seem unimportant, but it suggests a different kind of relationship between human beings and God. We sacrifice to God because we are in a relationship with God. We make sacrifices for God out of love, just like we make sacrifices—time, money, emotional energy, and much more—for the people we love. This framework for understanding the role of sacrifices helps us uncover insights in Leviticus on ways to use and understand the meaningful rituals in our religious practices.

The Book of Numbers is all about the journey through the wilderness from Egypt to the Promised Land. In the Torah, this journey is a physical one. The Israelites remain there for forty years. But it is not only a physical journey. It is also a spiritual one. Slavery does not trap only the body. It captures the mind and heart. It took a journey of forty years to turn the Israelites from forced slaves of Pharaoh to willing followers of God. One of my rabbinic mentors captured this truth in a quip: It took four days, he said, to get the Israelites out of Egypt. It took forty years to get the spirit of Egypt out of the Israelites.

Many of us undergo a similar spiritual journey. We may grow up with a narrow view of our own possibilities. We may feel trapped in a secular or religious worldview imposed by others. We may even become slaves to addictions. The Hebrew word for Egypt is *mitzrayim*. The same word also means "narrow places." The journey of the Book of Numbers guides us in our journey to a deep and wide faith and self-understanding.

The final book of the Torah is Deuteronomy. Deuteronomy does not add much to the narrative story of the Torah. It consists primarily of a recollection by Moses of the journey of the Israelites through the wilderness. Moses is preparing the Jewish people for their arrival and survival in the Promised Land. He will no longer be with them. His words, therefore, constitute his legacy. He is teaching the Israelites how to preserve the sacred message God revealed to them.

Are we leaving a meaningful legacy? All of us leave a legacy. Our lives are remembered by those who come after us. Having conducted almost a thousand funerals as a rabbi, I know the legacies we leave can feel painful, extraordinary, and everything in between. I have also learned that we can be conscious about the kind of legacy we seek to leave. Deuteronomy guides us in doing so. We will look at key verses where Moses conveys to the Israelites what matters most in carrying on the message God revealed to them. Given that Judaism survives to this day—and that it provided the context and foundation in which Christianity emerged—we can say Moses was successful in doing so.

By reading this book, you will find new ways to bring Torah wisdom into your life. You will also experience the Torah not simply as the Old Testament and the preamble to the New Testament, but as something far greater. For many centuries, the Old Testament was seen that way. Even among the many church groups where I have spoken, it is still sometimes seen in that way. It is perceived as the opening act for a main speaker and message.

I don't begrudge those who hold this view. Yet, in my experience, it minimizes the depth of our faith and the closeness we can feel with the God who created us all. Our understanding of God's word is incomplete without knowledge and study of the Torah. This book is your walk through the Torah. May its uncovering of our shared heritage bless us with wisdom.

CHAPTER 2

GENESIS

Genesis tells the story of the creation of the world. But most of its chapters are devoted to the creation and maintenance of families. Families are the foundation of human life, and Genesis portrays them in both their messiness and their beauty. Even though the families of Genesis may look and feel different from ours, the challenges they face echo our own. While the technology and structures of the world in which we live have changed, human nature has not. The same sibling rivalries, parental conflict, and need for forgiveness found in Genesis present themselves to us today.

We will learn what lessons Genesis yields for us by highlighting key verses, revealing the backstories behind them, and then drawing from insights and interpretations of the ancient and modern Jewish sages. Each verse frames a mini life lesson of sorts, focused on the relationships that mean the most to us. At the end of the chapter, you will find other verses that space did not permit us to include, as well as more guiding questions to deepen and widen the application of their teachings.

THE IMAGE OF GOD

In the image of God He created him;
male and female He created them.
Genesis 1:27

My mom spent her life teaching children with learning disabilities. She tutored them in our home, and I remember becoming increasingly frustrated by all the students constantly coming in and out. I must have been about eight or nine when I asked why she kept doing this. It was tiring. It required long hours. And though I did not know this then, the pay was not that great.

What she told me has stayed with me and may have even helped me find my calling. She said that every person was unique. Every person was made by God to be the way they are. Every child, she said, has God inside of them. She wanted to help them figure that out.

What my mom said echoes this extraordinary verse from the first chapter of Genesis. It is certainly among the most significant and influential biblical verses. Every human being is created in the image of God. My mom's words reveal one of the ways this verse shapes human life. But before looking at some of the other ways, let's step back and see the context in which this verse emerged and what it means.

Most people groups of the ancient Near East did not hold human equality as a value. Hammurabi's famous legal code—which dates to around 1750 BCE—inflicted a graver punishment for the murder of an aristocrat than it did for the murder of a commoner. Some human beings had inherently greater worth, based either on their family lineage, their class or social status, or other factor. Some societies still hold this ideal, and until slavery was abolished in the modern world, almost every country did.

In its very first chapter, however, the Torah challenges this belief. What makes us human beings, it teaches, is the spark of God within us. We may look different. We may think differently. We make come from different backgrounds and speak different languages. But within us is a reflection of God.

The Jewish sages use a wonderful parable to illustrate this idea. A Jewish coin maker was talking with a Roman guard. The guard challenged him and said, "Your God has no power. You do the same thing God does. God makes people. You make coins. What's the difference?" The coin maker responded, "When I mint coins, they all come out the same. But when God makes human beings, we all come out different." These types of parables are not meant to be taken literally. Sometimes they strike us as odd and outrageous. But they capture underlying truths. We all have one maker who made us unique. In fact, the parts of ourselves that are different—our unique traits or sense of identity— may well be God's signature.

How does this idea help families? Well, families are made up of unique human beings. And we do not choose the family into which we are born. We may wish our family members were different, but harmony depends on accepting the uniqueness in others. Conflict emerges when we try to make a person be someone they are not. God loves every human being as they are because every human being is created in the divine image. We all have that same capacity.

When we accept the uniqueness of each other in a family, however, we move closer to a core Torah value known *shalom bayit*, which means "peace in the home." The story of Adam and Eve illustrates one way they draw from our verse in deepening their relationship. This positive aspect of the story of the garden of Eden is often overlooked, but it gives a view into how our relationships provide some comfort and salve in a broken world. In other words, exile from the garden of Eden provides a context in which Adam and Eve grow closer to each other.

The Hebrew language makes this clear through some subtle wordplay. In chapter 2 of Genesis, we read of Eve's creation from the rib of Adam. When he first sees her, Adam responds with the words,

> *This one at last Is bone of my bones*
> *And flesh of my flesh.*
> *This one shall be called Woman [ishah],*
> *For from man [ish] was she taken.*
> Genesis 2:23

Adam's words reveal a nuance lost in the English translation. In Hebrew there are two words for man: *adam* and *ish*. *Adam* is a more technical and scientific word for "man." It is like our word "homo sapiens." *Adam* is connected to the word *adamah*, which means earth. The word *adam* reflects a view of human beings as simply a biological reality without a soul.

The word *ish*, however, conveys a different idea. An *ish* is a distinct person, a human being with a personality and uniqueness. An *ish* is an individual, not just a member of a biological species. We often overlook this nuance in the Hebrew because we are used to the English name "Adam." But in Hebrew *adam* is a generic word. *Ish* conveys an individual personality.[1]

Now why does this matter in the context of this verse and our relationships? Well, until this verse, we have only heard the word *Adam* in relation to the first human being. Until this moment, *Adam* has simply been a biological reality, not an individual with a soul. Only after the creation of Eve—only after *Adam* says the word *ishah*, the feminine version of the word *ish* and a word that also means a distinct unique personality—does *Adam* become *ish*. In other words, only in relation to other people does our full personality and humanity emerge. God creates us to live in relationship. That capacity is part of what makes us human. It reflects the divine image within us.

Jewish tradition carries this idea into many other teachings. One rabbinic sage compared a family dining table to the sacred altar that once stood in the Temple. When we connect with our loved ones in relationship, we bring the divine presence into our lives, just as the ancient priests invoked God's presence in the Jerusalem Temple. Relationships begin with seeing the spark of God in one another.

CAIN AND ABEL

*Cain set upon his brother Abel and
killed him.*

Genesis 4:8

Consider this truth: the first sibling relationship results in murder. Recognizing this may give us perspective on the challenges we face in our own relationships. But the story is much deeper than simply anger and jealousy between two brothers. Rather, it is about communication and the ways we deal with internal anger.

Cain and Abel each bring an offering to God. These offerings reflected their identities. Cain, the Torah tells us, is a "tiller of the soil." In other words, he is a farmer. Abel is a "keeper of sheep." In other words, he is a shepherd. Thus, Cain offers crops as his sacrifice to God. And Abel offers "the choicest of the firstlings of his flock." God prefers Abel's sacrifice. After Cain sees this, he murders Abel. God then sentences Cain to a life of wandering (Genesis 4:1-16).

Some biblical scholars interpret this story as an enactment of the conflict between nomadic and agrarian civilizations, between settled tribes and wandering ones. They fought over limited resources. That may well be true, but the story is also a profound family drama. We can see part of what went wrong— and what would have made for a different scenario— when we look at this exact verse where Cain kills Abel.

Prior to this verse, we know that God has warned Cain to control his anger. In one of the Torah's great example of literary personification, we read "Sin crouches at the door...You can be its master." But Cain does not. Instead, we come upon the fateful verse, "Cain said to his brother Abel...and when they were in the field, Cain set upon his brother Abel and killed him" (verses 7-8). This verse is confusing. It begins by saying "Cain said to his brother," but then it doesn't say what Cain said! Now certain translations of the Hebrew fill in the gap by supplying what Cain said: "Cain said to his brother, 'let us go to into the field,'" or something similar. But I believe the gap is intentional! It implies that Cain did not really speak to Abel. He did not express his anger and frustration. He did not communicate at all. Real communication between Cain and Abel might have averted the murder. The Torah makes that possibility clear in a later story about Joseph and his brothers. We will examine that story in detail later, but there is a moment when the brothers plan to kill Joseph. And then they talk about it, and revise their plans. This communication seems to help them become more aware of their emotions and moderate their plans. The same thing could have happened between Cain and Abel. But Cain was unable to do so.

The Torah suggests a reason why Cain did not communicate. He didn't listen! He didn't listen to God's warning to think through his actions. According to the Jewish sages, Cain didn't listen to Abel's pleas either. The sages said that after God preferred Abel's offering to Cain's, Abel sought to make peace and share his bounty with Cain. But Cain did not listen. His anger consumed him. He couldn't hear the voices of others. And he couldn't speak to them either. He closed himself off, and he lashed out in anger.

Sometimes all of us feel like Cain. We just don't want to listen. We think the world is out to get us. We are so tired or frustrated that we can't speak. And we feel justified in our anger. Look at the story from Cain's perspective. Both he and his brother made an offering from their possessions. In fact, the text suggests that Cain was the one who made the first offering. Abel followed him. But for reasons that are not obvious, God preferred Abel's offering. We can see why Cain would be angry. He feels rejected by God.

That can happen to us as well, especially within families. Spouses can feel ignored or rejected. Siblings can feel one parent favors the other. We all know the feeling of rejection, even when it was unintentional. As a parent of two young children, I frequently hear one or the other saying, "Why aren't you listening to me?" or "Why does Hannah get to do it and not me?" Responding to each child's individual needs and trying to do the right thing can lead to unintended consequences.

How do we respond to feelings of rejection? And how should we listen and speak to avoid engendering that feeling in others? We learn one way to respond when we think about the context in which this story takes place. Cain and Abel represent the first generation born outside of the garden of Eden. They are living in a broken world with pain and suffering, and sometimes they do not see why that pain and struggle characterizes their reality. We know from our own experience that we can't always see why bad things happen. But Cain seems not to understand this truth. Perhaps this story serves as a reminder to us not to expect the world to operate with perfect justice. We cannot always know and discern God's ways. Sometimes acceptance of ambivalence matters more than certainty. Cain can't handle the uncertainty. But if we are to live with some measure of wholeness and peace, we must. One way of coping with uncertainty is to express our hurt and anger. Cain could have done this to God. He could have said "God, why did you reject my sacrifice. I offered myself to you. And you humiliated me. Why?" Or Cain could have said, "I feel despondent and angry, God. You rejected me. Please help me cope." In other parts of the Bible, this plaintive calling out to God is normal. Think of Job questioning his fate and Abraham arguing with God over the fate of Sodom and Gomorrah. But Cain says nothing. He does not invite God into his frustration.

Sometimes we do the same thing with our loved ones. We let anger and frustration fester. When I prepare to marry a couple, I ask them to go through a series of questions with each other. There are about thirty-five of them. Then I tell them to pick the three questions that sparked the most discussion. At our next meeting, we discuss their conversations around those three questions. One of the questions is "What makes you angry at each other? Describe an experience where one of you hurt the other." Almost every couple selects this question as one of the three we discuss. The conversations that ensue from it help them understand and better support each other.

This truth may seem counterintuitive. Some happy couples say they never fight with each other. But experience tells me this cannot be exactly right. It suggests to me that one of them is hiding or ignoring what hurts them. And knowing what hurts a spouse or a friend or a sibling is part of what binds us together. In other words, intimacy requires depth, and depth includes knowing each other well—including things that spark anger or pain.

A nineteenth-century Jewish folktale captured this truth. Two friends were sitting in a bar. They had a bit too much to drink, and their altered state led them to discuss things they had never talked about before. One turned to the other and asked, "Do you love me?" He responded, "Of course I love you. We've known each other our whole lives." The first friend then replied, "Tell me, then, what hurts me?" The second friend responded, "How do I know what hurts you?" The first friend answered, "How can you love me if you don't know what hurts me?"

I would say that to know what hurts those we love, we have to listen, and we have to speak. Cain did not do either.

GO FORTH

The LORD *said to Abram, "Go forth from*
your native land and from your father's
house to the land that I will show you."

Genesis 12:1

These words are the first God speaks to Abraham. They begin the journey that led to the beginning of Judaism, and then ultimately Christianity and the Western world as we know it today. Along with their universal historical importance, they are also deeply personal. God is inviting Abraham to leave his family and homeland. God is inviting Abraham to trust in God's promise and journey to an unknown destination. God's call, however, is even more than that. It is an invitation to begin the journey every human being undergoes. That is the journey to self-discovery, differentiation, and maturity. While it may seem from this verse that this journey is purely about separating oneself from one's family, it is much more subtle and complex than that. Each of us can learn from Abraham's journey and the insights of the Jewish sages. The journey includes four steps.

The first is faith. Abraham has to have faith in the message God reveals to him. In Hebrew the word for faith also includes trust. The word is *emunah*. The best translation is not "faith," but "faithfulness." The journey requires a faithfulness to the promise God makes.

While we may not hear the voice of God directly in the same way Abraham did, we also need faith to make the journey of our own lives. Without faith, we are simply a series of chemicals interacting with one another. We are, as atheist scientist Richard Dawkins put it, a collection of selfish genes. Why should we take a risk to leave our comfortable environment? Why should we not simply follow our own impulses?

Without faith, we don't have free will. We are simply preprogrammed animals. Some of the world's leading atheists like Sam Harris use neuroscience to try to prove this idea.

Growing up requires faith. We need faith in the words of those who are raising us. We need faith that life is worth living. The truth is that we all have faith. What differentiates us is where that faith leads us to journey.

That truth brings us to the second step: leave-taking. Every journey requires us to leave what is comfortable and familiar, at least temporarily. Abraham leaves his father's house. Moses leaves the land of Egypt where he was born, and then he leaves the land of Midian where he had found refuge. The patriarch Jacob—whom we will discuss again later this chapter—leaves his homeland and journeys to the home of his uncle Laban.

Leave-taking is significant because it is a critical component of encountering God. The Bible illustrates this idea over and over again. This leave-taking is not always physical, as it is in the case of Abraham. It can be psychological or spiritual as well. It is recognizing that, as Paul writes in the book of 1 Corinthians, we have to leave behind "childish ways" and reorient our being if we want to experience God (1 Corinthians 13:11). No one can tell us the exact way this will happen. But it must.

And when it does, we, paradoxically, realize that leave-taking is not a total break with everything that happened before. Rather, leave-taking connects us with what has been inside of us all along. Once again, Abraham's journey reflects this truth. Our first clue to this insight is in the first words of the Torah portion itself. The Hebrew words translated as "leave" in the verse above are *lech lecha*. *Lech lecha* means "go forth," but the grammar also suggests it means, "go into yourself." Abraham's journey is as much about uncovering the ideas that are already inside of him as it is an experience of growth and change.

When we look closely at the text, we also see that Abraham's journey began even before God called out to him. Abraham's story doesn't begin with Abraham. It begins with Abraham's father Terah. Terah is born in Ur of the Chaldeans. They live there. It is Terah who leaves for the land of Canaan and stops in Haran on the way. Terah dies in Haran. Abraham (his name here is still Abram) and his wife Sarah (her name here is still Sarai) are already on their way to the Promised Land when God calls out to him. His call was to affirm the journey begun by his father, but to do so in his own way. He continued and extended what happened before him.

So do we all. We are who we are because of the people who shaped and influenced us. No one is born a blank slate. Even when our journey takes us in a radical new direction from our parents and ancestors, we are imprinted with their marks and memories. How we use and interpret those marks and memories is up to us. The Torah makes clear that children do not inherit the sins of their parents. God does not punish us for what others have done. Yet, however we view the lives and values of those who came before us, they still shaped our character, for better or for worse. Our journey may take a different path, but it starts somewhere that's determined by those who preceded us. As the great writer William Faulkner said, "The past is never dead. It's not even past."[2]

With that in mind, we come to the final part of the journey: leaving a legacy. From the very beginning of Abraham's journey, God makes a promise: your descendants will inherit the Promised Land, and they will be as numerous as the stars in the sky. Abraham knew his journey did not end with him. It continued through his descendants. We see direct evidence of this near the end of his life. Among his foremost tasks is finding a wife for his son Isaac. He succeeds. Our legacy is not, however, purely about having children. It is about passing on values. It is keeping our memories alive through the lives of others.

Abraham and Sarah, of course, did this through the creation of a new religion and nation. Each of us, however, can do so in ways big and small. One technique I recommend is based on a thousand-year-old medieval Jewish practice. It is writing an "ethical will." An ethical will is not about money. It is about the values, experiences, and life lessons we leave for our descendants. Even though it comes from God and is given later to Moses, we might say the Torah is Abraham's ethical will. It lays out his life experiences, values, and practices God imparted to him through the formation of a new people.

RIVALRY

When Esau heard his father's words, he
burst into wild and bitter sobbing, and
said to his father, "Bless me too, Father!"

But he [Isaac] answered, "Your brother
came with guile and took away your
blessing."

[Esau] said, "Was he, then, named
Jacob that he might supplant me these
two times? First he took away my
birthright and now he has taken away my
blessing!" And he added, "Have you not
reserved a blessing for me?"

Genesis 27:34-36

The theme of sibling rivalry begun with Cain
and Abel extends throughout the Book of Genesis.
Abraham's two sons, Ishmael and Isaac, do not directly
quarrel, but they are separated shortly after Isaac is
born. Isaac's two sons, Jacob and Esau, begin their lives
in tension. They are twins, and Jacob is born holding
on to Esau's heel. The implication of the text is that he
wanted to leave his mother's womb first. His Hebrew
name—*Yaakov*—means heel. Their tensions continue
into adulthood. The twins are opposite in character.

Esau, we read, is an outdoorsman. Jacob spends his
time inside. According to the Jewish sages, Esau is a
man of the earth. Jacob is a man of the book. Esau
is his father's favorite. Their mother, Rebecca, prefers

Jacob. The first time we see the brothers interact is a time of conflict.

Esau has just finished hunting. But he has not succeeded in securing any meat. He arrives home and tells his brother he is starving and asks for some of Jacob's lentil soup. Jacob agrees on the condition that Esau sell him his birthright, that is, the status of the firstborn son. Esau agrees, reasoning that he is about to die if he doesn't eat, and what good is the birthright if he is dead. Esau eats and drinks, and the brothers separate.

We see them again as their father is about to die. Isaac tells Esau he would like to taste some of his meat before he dies. When Esau delivers him the meat, Isaac will give him the blessing of the firstborn son. Isaac's wife, Rebecca, overhears the plan. She wants Jacob to receive the blessing instead of Esau. While the Torah does not state clearly what the blessing entails, the Jewish sages say it marks the child who will carry on the covenant of Abraham. The blessing of the firstborn marks the child preferred by God. Rebecca sees it as her duty to ensure Jacob receives that blessing.

She prepares the meat Isaac likes, tells Jacob to dress in Esau's clothes (Isaac is nearly blind, so he wouldn't see Jacob's head or body), and then instructs him to deliver the meal to Isaac and receive the firstborn blessing. Jacob complies. Isaac wavers in bestowing the blessing, saying to himself that the "voice is the voice of Jacob." Yet he does so.

Jacob then leaves and Esau arrives shortly thereafter. When Isaac tells him what happened, Esau cries. His words resonate with us. Esau has been deceived. Esau has been wronged. And there is nothing he can do to fix it. His own brother—with the cooperation of his mother—wanted and then took what was rightfully Esau's. This sibling conflict is more complex than the others we have seen. First, the parents are involved and one even complicit in the deceit. Second, the tension remains unresolved. Esau cries out. Esau is wronged. But Jacob quickly disappears and leaves town to go live with his uncle Laban. Esau has vowed to murder him, but the Torah shifts focus to Jacob's life with Laban, and the tension between the brothers lingers.

What can the Torah be teaching us here? On one level, the Torah is advancing its theological purpose. Jacob is the one God has chosen to carry on the covenant. This story shows the way God arranged for that to happen. But on a relational level, the layers of meaning and potential lessons in this story abound. First, we can identify with Esau because we know what it's like to be ignored or victimized. We remember the time we did not get the reward we deserved. We remember being tricked or getting punished for something we didn't do. We may even have experiences where a sibling deliberately undermined our relationship with our mom and dad. Esau is a stand-in for feelings we experience.

Esau's fate also helps us the see the reality and dangers of parental favoritism. In this case of Jacob and Esau, the two are so different that it seems each parent naturally gravitated to the one to whom they felt closest. Thus, the conflict between the two brothers played out between the parents. Rebecca may not only have felt close to Jacob. Perhaps she sensed that he had the greater potential to carry on the covenant. Perhaps she felt he was simply the better child, and it was her duty to take advantage of Isaac's blindness to get Jacob what he wanted.

This kind of favoritism is not uncommon today. I remember a couple in my first synagogue who had two children—an older daughter and a younger son. We were preparing for the daughter's bat mitzvah ceremony. I was getting to know the family, and I asked if she had siblings. At that point, the conversation shifted, and all the parents began talking about was their son. What a great athlete he was! How good in school he did! How he was going to participate in his sister's bat mitzvah service! I struggled with how to respond in an empathetic way, but it became clear the parents found it much easier to take pride in and show affection to their son. The story of Jacob and Esau shows the dangers of this tendency. Not only do the parent's actions lead the brothers to a twenty-year feud and Esau's desire to murder his brother, we even see both children distance themselves from their parents. Jacob does not see his mother ever again, and the Torah seems to suggest he does not see his father again either before Isaac dies. Esau leaves home as well and marries someone from the tribe of one of Israel's enemies, the Hittites, gravely disappointing his parents. Unchecked favoritism can destroy families.

In the end, the Torah gives us some guidance in how to reconcile and prevent such conflicts from persisting. Esau does receive a blessing from his father. The blessing suggests he will live a fulfilling life, and he will not be permanently subordinate to his brother. The Jewish sages elaborate on Esau's fate and suggest that the Messiah will not arrive until the world hears the cry of Esau! This is their way of suggesting that Esau will eventually receive justice. God does not allow injustice to persist forever. And Jacob does not get off scot-free from his behavior. In the same way Jacob tricked his brother, Jacob's uncle Laban deceives him. He substitutes his older daughter for the younger daughter Jacob seeks to marry, and then makes Jacob work for him for fourteen years so that he can marry the daughter he promised him.

In addition, Jacob and Esau reconcile in a stunning way. After Jacob finishes his time serving Laban and begins his journey back to Canaan, he learns that Esau has gathered four hundred soldiers and plans to meet him. Jacob is terrified. He divides his family into two halves, hoping that if one is attacked by Esau, the other will survive. He spends the night before the encounter wrestling with an angel. Then the two brothers meet, speak kind words to the other, and go their separate ways. What led to the healing between the two?

Well, one simple answer is time. Sometimes conflicts fade over time, and we realize they haven't hurt us in the way we thought. But in my experience, the opposite can also be true. Time sometimes solidifies conflict. In the case of Jacob and Esau, time is not the critical factor. Two other realities help explain the reconciliation, and they both can guide us as well.

The first is Jacob's self-awareness. The Jacob of twenty years ago is not the Jacob of today. He has experienced twenty years of forced servitude to Laban (Genesis 31:38). He is married with children. He has wrestled with an angel who left him with a permanent injury. Perhaps the wounds of life changed him from an arrogant, deceitful young man to a wiser, more empathic leader. He embodies a truth later stated in the Book of Ecclesiastes: Time and chance befall us all (see Ecclesiastes 9:11). Like Jacob, we can draw from our painful life experiences to open our hearts to others.

The second factor is Esau's capacity to forgive. As we know, Esau has experienced deep pain. But the Torah tells us that he runs up to Jacob, without reservation, and embraces him! Jacob has prepared an elaborate ritual to show his respect for Esau, and seemingly tries to bribe him with expensive gifts. But Esau is not interested. He simply wants to see and hug his brother.

What explains Esau's capacity to forgive? I think we find the answer by looking back at his first interaction with Jacob, when Jacob forces Esau to give him the status of the firstborn son for a bowl of lentil soup. While Esau may have starved to death had he not given up the status, he does not seem to mind terribly. We read nothing about him lodging a protest later. It seems he is just fine giving up the status and forgetting about it. This suggests Esau has a capacity to quickly put the past behind him. He does not let anger linger. He moves on.

This capacity to move forward is a tremendous gift. Some people have it naturally, but we can all work at it. Now some might say we should never forget, that forgetting that someone hurt us is a way of condoning it and just makes us a glutton for punishment. Forgetting, however, does not imply condoning. Forgetting here means moving on. It means not holding ourselves hostage to the past. It means remembering differently in order to serve a deeper purpose. This capacity is especially important for those who have survived traumatic experience. A recent scientific study at the University of Texas showed that "to intentionally forget is to remember differently, on purpose. Importantly, for scientists and therapists, intentional forgetting also may be an ability that can be practiced and deliberately strengthened."[3] More than three thousand years ago, Esau taught us this truth. His story gives hope to any of us who have survived trauma within our family.

JOSEPH AND HIS FATHER

Trauma can often manifest itself in later generations. Jealousy and anger can reappear. And it does in the lives of Jacob's children. He has twelve of them, and the most prominent is Joseph. The story of Joseph and his brothers is a well-known one. It is a story that ends in a beautiful moment of reconciliation, which we will examine in this section. But there is another, subtle conflict in the story of Joseph. It is the one between Joseph and his father, Jacob. This tension is not obvious on a surface-level reading, but we see hints throughout the text. It is this relationship we will explore and look at what it can teach us today.

Joseph comes into the world as his father's favorite son, because he is the son of Jacob's favored wife, Rachel. Jacob showers Joseph with affection. Most famously, he gives him a special garment, often known as the coat of many colors, which angers his brothers. They clearly understood their father favored Joseph, and Joseph amplified their hostility by describing to them several dreams in which he rules over them. The second of these dreams is quite revealing.

As Joseph describes it to his brothers: "I had another dream, and this time the sun and moon and eleven stars were bowing down to me." Joseph then describes his dream to his father, and Jacob grows angry because Jacob immediately understands the symbolism of this dream. The sun and the moon are Joseph's father and mother, Jacob and Rachel. The eleven stars are Joseph's brothers. Jacob rebukes Joseph. Though the Torah does not explain Jacob's anger, the clear implication is that Jacob finds it outrageous for Joseph to suggest that his mother and father bow before, especially since his mother is dead. His brothers serving him is one thing. His elderly father and dead mother is another. Joseph, it seems, has gone too far in his visions of grandeur.

Shortly thereafter, Jacob sends Joseph to go and help his brothers in the field. When he arrives, Joseph's brothers take him, throw him in a pit, and then sell him to traveling slave traders. Ultimately, as we know, Joseph becomes prime minister of Egypt, rising from a slave to the pharaoh's right-hand man, and his ingenuity saves

Egypt and his entire family from famine. But there is a glaring question pulsating through Joseph's rise in Egyptian life. He never seeks to contact his father. He never even sends couriers to check on him. Once he is prime minister of Egypt, he clearly has the means to do so. But Joseph does nothing. And we know from the text that Jacob believes Joseph is dead, and he falls into a depression after Joseph's brothers tell him a wild animal tore Joseph to pieces. So why doesn't Joseph reach out and tell his father he is okay? At the very least, why does Joseph not even check on his father to make sure he is alive?

The answer, I believe, is that Joseph believes his father has rejected him. He believes his father no longer wanted to see him. Why else would Jacob have sent Joseph to help his brothers in the field? He had to have known that Joseph's brothers despised him. He also knew Joseph's brothers were capable of violence. Earlier in the Torah, they had destroyed an entire town in revenge for an offense against their sister Dinah (Genesis 34). Jacob had also broken off contact with other children before. When Reuben, his oldest son, sleeps with one of Jacob's concubines, Jacob cuts him off (Genesis 35:22; see also Genesis 49:3-4 and 1 Chronicles 5:1-2). Thus, Joseph could reasonably assume that his father was punishing him for his vision of ruling over him. His father, Joseph concluded, had sent him to the field to get beaten and sold by his brothers.

Indeed, shortly after he marries an Egyptian and has his first child, Joseph reveals how relieved he is to be out of his father's house and to have escaped from his past. As we read, Joseph named the first-born Manasseh, meaning, "God has made me forget completely my hardship and my parental home" (Genesis 41:51). Joseph felt rejected by his father, and as he established a new life in Egypt, he finally felt relief. He did not want any connection to his past.

But this, as we will soon see, was a distorted vision of the past. Joseph could not have been more wrong. His father did not despise him. His father mourned for him. His father longed for him. Eventually, as we will see, Joseph realizes the error of his ways. But Joseph's assumptions about his father's feelings led him to not speak or express concern about him for twenty-two years.

In what way does this story offer wisdom to us today? Over and over again, we imagine the way another person is feeling. We imagine their anger, their disappointment, their dislike. Have you ever looked at someone talking and laughing and imagined they are talking about you? We all do this, and that misperception can carry over into negative feelings and misinterpreting what people do. These misinterpretations can destroy longstanding relationships. We might think our spouse is angry at us when they just had a bad day at work. We might think a driver deliberately cut us off in traffic when they may be on their way to the hospital. Sometimes misunderstandings can lead to prolonged conflict. In the film *Avalon*, there is a magnificent scene during a family Thanksgiving meal, where the relatives who still live in the city are late arriving in the suburbs for dinner. The family in the suburbs had lots of children, and they cut the turkey and began eating because the kids were crying. When the city relatives arrive and see that they have already started eating, they feel rejected, leave, and the family falls apart.

Is there a way out of misunderstandings? Forgiveness is not the answer in these cases because forgiveness usually involves deliberate hurt. Misunderstandings cannot always be avoided. The most effective way to counter it is empathy. In the case of Joseph, Judah's impassioned plea to him helps him recognize Jacob's true feelings toward him (Genesis 44). When he realizes how much his father has suffered and missed him, he instantly recognizes he was wrong. When Joseph could feel his father's feelings, his own feelings changed. Empathy is the bridge to understanding.

The nineteenth-century Jewish writer Isaac Loeb Peretz relates this truth in a humorous and profound story about a wagon driver and his horse. The two were always at odds. The horse would say: "First feed me the oats, and then I will pull the wagon." The driver would answer: "First pull the wagon, and then I will feed you the oats." The driver was the one with the whip, and he would use it until the horse gave in. Finally, the horse dropped dead.

Now the driver was forced to pull the wagon by himself. This took more strength than the driver had, and soon he, too, collapsed and died. When the driver arrived in heaven, he was informed that the horse had filed a complaint against him. He was summoned to appear for a trial before the Throne of Judgment. The horse testified: "He beat me unmercifully! He thrashed the life out of me with his whip!" The driver retorted: "He's just a horse, and a lousy one at that. I only used the whip because he wouldn't move!" "But I hadn't the strength," cried the horse. "Did I have the strength," shouted the driver. "I had to pull the wagon myself. Is a horse not stronger than a man?"

The Heavenly Court was in a quandary. It deliberated quite a while before rendering its verdict: "The horse will not listen to the driver, and the driver will not listen to the horse. Therefore, both will return to earth. The horse will become a driver, and the driver will become a horse. The heavenly court will wait until they learn to hear each other's voice and learn to feel each other's pain." We can do the same for one another.

RECONCILIATION

Genesis begins with sibling murder. It ends with sibling forgiveness. The story of Genesis, in many ways, is the story and struggle to build and sustain a family. It is the story of a group of people who learn, slowly and haltingly, to embrace and shape their laws toward God's word.

By the end of the Book of Genesis, this shaping of family relationships finds a powerful expression. The man who had tried to escape his past sees his ultimate return to it. As he is dying, Joseph tells his sons they must eventually take his bones out of Egypt. They will return, he says, to the land of Canaan. When they do so, they must carry his bones with them.

This request is more than it seems on the surface. It is not purely about Joseph's bones. Presumably, the Israelites will not leave Egypt for a long time. (They do so over four hundred years later.) By that time, Joseph's bones will not be solid anymore. They will be dust. But they symbolize the reconciliation and indelible ties of the children of Jacob. They represent the process by which the Jewish people grew from a series of tribes in conflict—the frequent sibling rivalries—to a unified nation. This coming together made possible the next book of the Torah, the Book of Exodus, because it is in Exodus that the nation of Israel experiences God and becomes a holy people. They had to become a family before they could become a nation. And when they become a nation, they receive a sacred message—the Torah—that changes history. It is to that journey that we now turn.

CHAPTER 3

EXODUS

The English names we use for the Bible do not always match the Hebrew ones. The Hebrew name is always the first significant word of the book. (Significant means not "the," "these," "and," or "or.") The English name *Exodus* captures one of the themes of this book: the freeing of Israel from slavery in Egypt and the journey to the Promised Land. The Hebrew name, however, is less dramatic. It is *shemot*, "names." The Book of Exodus begins with the words, "These are the *names*" of the Israelites who went down to Egypt with Jacob. As such, we name the book *Shemot*, names.

While exodus is a primary theme of this book, the name *Shemot* (pun intended) hints at another theme, a consistent thread running through the Book of Exodus. In Exodus the Israelites make a name for themselves, becoming a people as they hear God's voice at Mount Sinai. Moses undergoes the same process. They discover their identity by listening to God's voice and responding to it. Hearing the divine name—which Moses does at the burning bush—represents the beginning of their salvation.

The process by which Moses and the Israelites make a name for themselves can guide us in shaping and understanding the way we identify and see ourselves. Identities are not automatically given. They are a combination of what we are given and what we do. We may not undergo all the experiences and plagues the Israelites did. We may not have to journey in the wilderness for forty years. But we do pass through times of sorrow and times of joy. We do experience loss and miracles. Through them, we grow and shape who we are. We write and experience our salvation story.

A PHARAOH AROSE
WHO KNEW NOT JOSEPH

*A new king arose over Egypt who did
not know Joseph.*

Exodus 1:8

The drama begins quickly in the Book of Exodus. We learn that all of Joseph's family came to Egypt and settled there. They lived comfortably for a while. Then a new pharaoh arose. This is another way of saying that the ruler of Egypt does not know the history of the Jewish people in Egypt. He does not know of their role in saving Egypt. In other words, the country has historical amnesia. It no longer knows its past.

As a result, the Egyptians begin to see the Israelites as a treacherous people. They are like a fifth column ready to aid Egypt's enemies. To avoid this imagined scenario, they enslave the Israelites. They then plan a massive genocide, murdering every Israelite male at birth. This is the darkest hour the Jewish people have yet experienced. Yet, it also marks a turning point. That process begins almost immediately after Pharaoh's enslavement decree, as we read, "The people [Israelites] multiplied..." The Jewish sages also teach that as the Jewish people multiplied, they never stopped speaking Hebrew. The Egyptians tried to force them to stop. But they refused. Then the Egyptians tried to keep husbands and wives apart so they could not reproduce. But they did. Over and over again the Jewish sages echo the idea that the context of slavery actually strengthened and grew the Jewish people.

How is that possible? The Torah recognizes that with faith, we grow in periods of trial and discomfort. When we know God is with us, we respond to a sense of urgency. This is not always true for everybody. And sometimes we cannot see evidence of it. Sometimes it feels like we are lost and despondent when facing tragedy. And sometimes we are. But the Book of Exodus echoes this truth over and over again: out of the darkness we find light. Let's look at the way the Jewish people do so and what we can learn from them.

The first way, as we noted, is strengthening their own sense of self. We all have a past that preceded our birth. Our lives emerge in a context shaped by the ones who gave us birth, raised us, and helped form who we are. The exodus is the context for the birth of the Jewish people. We see this truth echoed clearly in the opening words of the Ten Commandments (Exodus 20:2). God's first words are, "I the LORD am your God who brought you out of the land of Egypt, the house of bondage." These are words God is addressing to the entire Jewish people. The first way God introduces himself is by saying, I "brought you out of the land of Egypt"!

To understand what this means, imagine you are meeting a man you do not know. Perhaps you know his spouse. So you meet John and he says, "Hi, I'm John. I'm married to Robin." The first words John says are the signal by which you know him. It may also be what he thinks is his defining feature. Some people may introduce themselves and immediately tell you what they do for work. Others might tell you where they are from. When God introduces himself to the Jewish people, God says, I am the One who brought you out of the land of Egypt.

The exodus not only symbolizes the Israelite past. It also establishes a particular kind of context from which they emerged: one in which they experience persecution and challenge it in the name of divine justice. If there had not arisen a pharaoh "who did not know Joseph," the Jewish people may well not be here today. They may have remained a separate group within Egyptian culture for a while, but probably ultimately assimilated into the Egyptian people or been lost during one of the many wars in which Egypt was conquered. They were not a large group in Egypt. They could easily have been absorbed. This fate has happened to Jews and other religious minorities throughout history. But their adversity created solidarity. An overwhelming challenge built an extraordinary bond that became a core part of their identity.

We often grow closer to others in the midst of external challenges. During my first year of rabbinical school, my entire class spent the year in Israel. It was 2001–02, the height of the Second Intifada, when suicide-bombers exploded throughout Israel. We had at least one bombing a week in Jerusalem, where I lived. Yet despite all the fear and anxious parents, my class developed an extraordinary closeness to each other and a love of Israel. Living in the midst of terror helped us appreciate how important it was to support each other. Seeing the vulnerability of Israelis made us realize how precious Israel is and how brave an average Israeli has to be. The terrorism produced the opposite of its intent. Instead of causing despair, it built strength.

In addition to drawing the Israelites closer together, the experience of persecution established one of Judaism's core beliefs: God is on the side of the oppressed. God does not condone tyrants. God does not protect the powerful in the face of injustice. Today we may take this belief for granted. We live in a world shaped by the Bible. But three thousand years ago in Egypt, many believed the opposite: might made right. The pharaoh, many believed, was a god himself. What he deemed right had to be right. Slaves were ignored by the gods while the powerful were blessed by them.

Moses—and by extension, the entire Jewish people—challenged this worldview. When God says to Pharaoh through Moses, "Let My people go," God identifies with the oppressed. God upends an unjust system, and this experience reverberates through Jewish life. Repeatedly the Torah says, "You shall not oppress the stranger, for you were strangers in the land of Egypt." It is one of the most repeated commandments in the entire Bible. Had the Jewish people not undergone the rise of a pharaoh "who did not know Joseph" and experienced slavery, we would not have this central value. It helped us become, in Abraham Heschel's phrase, obsessed with justice.

Think about your core values: where did they come from? Some may have come from our parents or background. Others, however, grew out of life experience. My maternal grandfather, for example, grew up experiencing many health issues. He ultimately became the first in his family to go to college and then to medical school. He became a beloved doctor in Milwaukee for forty years. He never turned away someone who could not pay. He told me the doctors who took care of him led him to decide to commit to treating anyone in need. Life experience established his values, as it could do for us, and as it did for the Israelites more than three thousand years ago.

THREE EXPERIENCES OF MOSES

We begin to see foreshadowing of the values that would shape the Jewish people in the early life of Moses. In other words, Moses's personal journey foreshadows the Israelites' communal journey. In three beautiful passages, the Torah encapsulates it. In much the same way as the Gospels establish Jesus's character through tests in the wilderness, God establishes Moses's character through tests in Egypt and Midian. Each test builds on the other.

The first happens when Moses leaves Pharaoh's palace. He comes across an Egyptian slave master beating an Israelite. He recognizes the Israelite as his kinsman. The Torah does not tell us how Moses knew he was himself an Israelite. Moses could have been led to believe he was an Egyptian since he was raised in Pharaoh's palace. The Torah never tells us whether Pharaoh or his daughter—the one who rescued Moses from the Nile River—ever told him he was an Israelite. Yet, when he leaves the palace, he immediately recognizes the Israelite as his kinsman. According to the Jewish sages, Pharaoh's daughter likely told him. This speaks to her righteousness and the truth that sometimes salvation and care come from a place where we least expect it. Pharaoh was the one who ordered the genocide of the Israelites. Who would expect Pharaoh's daughter to save the future Israelite leader? The sages think so highly of Pharaoh's daughter that they give her the name *Batya*, which means "daughter of God."

Interestingly, she is also one of several women who save Moses's life. The first two are his mother and his sister, Miriam. They develop and implement the plan to place him in a wicker basket and send him down the Nile River. Before that, the two midwives who deliver Moses (and the other Hebrew boys) also save his life by disobeying Pharaoh's instruction to kill the boys as soon as they are born (Exodus 1:15-21). These midwives were named Shiphrah and Puah, and it's unclear whether they were Egyptian women (that is, Egyptian midwives to the Hebrews) or Hebrew women (that is, Hebrew midwives). Whatever their identity, the Jewish sages consider the midwives especially heroic because they defied the pharaoh in the name of saving lives. One contemporary rabbi, Jonathan Sacks, even calls them the first exemplars of human rights. They engaged in civil disobedience to save innocent life.

Moses's first actions clearly illustrate the imprint of the values and character of those who saved his life. When he sees the Egyptian taskmaster beating the Israelite slave, the first thing he does is "look to his left and his right." On the surface, it seems Moses is looking around to make sure nobody will see what he is about to do. In other words, Moses is making sure no one will report his defending the Israelite slave. The Jewish sages, however, look at this verse differently. They say Moses was looking to see if anyone else was going to step in and defend the Israelite. He was looking for someone to act with justice. When he sees no one stepping up, he decides that he must. The Jewish sages draw an extraordinary lesson from this action, writing in the Talmud, "In a place where there are no human beings, you must be a human being." Moses acts for justice and compassion when no else will.

Moses's next action adds a nuance to the meaning of justice. After he defends the Israelite slave, he sees two Israelites fighting with one another. He challenges the aggressor. The aggressor says to Moses, "Who are you? Who made you our leader? Are you going to kill me like you did the Egyptian?" Moses here faces an extraordinary character challenge. Will he back down because the aggressor is one of his kinsmen? Will he permit injustice if it is someone from his side? Moses does not. He stops the aggressor and the conflict. He remains steadfast in his convictions and can withstand challenges to his values and leadership.

Moses recognizes, however, that word of his defense of the Israelite slave has spread. He must escape Egypt. He flees to the land of Midian, which was largely nomadic. His first encounter there takes place at a well. He witnesses a group of shepherds attacking seven sisters. He is a stranger. He has a relationship with neither party in this dispute. Yet, Moses steps in and defends the sisters. Analyzing this incident, the twentieth-century Jewish theologian Ahad Ha-am points out, "The prophet makes no distinction among persons apart from the distinction between right and wrong. [Moses] saw shepherds aggressively taking advantage of defenseless women and [as the Bible says] 'stood up and rescued them and watered their flock.'"[1] These three incidents illustrate Moses's inner impulse. They reflect his emerging identity. They prepare him for the call he is soon to receive.

Before we address that call, however, let us see what insight Moses's experience has for us. On the one hand, it shows one of the ways a Jewish passion for justice emerged. As the foremost prophet of the Jewish people, Moses is used by God to establish what beliefs and values matter most. But Moses's early life also teaches us that God speaks and calls to what we unconsciously desire. Moses had a passion for justice. Therefore, God put him in situations where he could exercise it. The Jewish sages teach that each of us experiences a moment where we realized "for which we were created." Moses experienced those moments as he heard God's call for justice. Part of our task is to listen for the moments when we do as well. They might not be as dramatic as Moses's. But they will reveal our character and the image of God implanted within us.

THE BUSH WAS NOT CONSUMED

An angel of the LORD *appeared to him*
in a blazing fire out of a bush. He gazed,
and there was a bush all aflame, yet the
bush was not consumed. Moses said, "I
must turn aside to look at this marvelous
sight; why doesn't the bush burn up?"
When the LORD *saw that he had turned*
aside to look, God called to him out of
the bush: "Moses! Moses!" He answered,
"Here I am."

Exodus 3:2-4

After defending the Midiante sisters, Moses marries one of them, and settles in Midian. He is living a simple life when God speaks to him once again. He encounters the burning bush. This is one of the most enigmatic and memorable moments of the Torah. It has led to a range of interpretations in both Jewish and Christian theology. One shared interpretation is that the burning bush illustrates the reality of miracles. Moses sees a miracle unfolding before him. It transforms him and leads him to become the leader of the Israelites. While I share this point of view, our focus here is the way the words of the Book of Exodus shaped the identity of the Jewish people and their ultimate salvation. Looking at this miraculous moment through a different lens helps us understand that process.

First, we need to see who Moses was when he arrives at the bush. He is at a critical turning point. After his escape into Midian, he had established a peaceful life for himself, marrying the daughter of a Midianite priest and working as a shepherd. We can imagine that Moses could have continued this peaceful existence. He had already lived a tumultuous life, having been saved from death when he was a baby, growing up in the Egyptian royal palace, and then avoiding death once again as a man on the run. Perhaps he had finally found the peace he had been looking for.

But God did not intend to leave Moses alone. God uses the miracle of the burning bush to waken Moses. After doing so, Moses is told that the one speaking to him from the bush is the God of his ancestors. God charges Moses to free the Israelites from Egypt.

Moses's initial reaction is concern. God is asking Moses to undergo a massive transformation. Even though he has just witnessed a miracle, Moses wonders if this is really God who is speaking to him. Then we see another more subtle miracle. It is the way God speaks to Moses. God spoke, the sages taught, in the voice of Moses's father. When Moses heard his father's voice, he turned and believed. It is in the act of listening to God's voice—revealed with the voice of Moses's father—that Moses awakens.

What can this interpretation possibly mean? Moses had not likely heard his father's voice since he was a baby. Moses, we remember, was shepherded by his mother and sister onto a raft and sent floating down the Nile River because Pharaoh was killing all male Israelite babies at the time of his birth. How could he truly know his father's voice? The sages, I think, are suggesting that Moses heard God's voice in the deepest recesses of his heart. God's voice struck a chord that had been implanted in him at birth. God's voice had an intimacy that only a father's or mother's voice could have. Only that kind of voice could have motivated Moses to change.

By understanding God's voice as having the timbre of Moses's father, the sages are also teaching that Moses felt a deep responsibility to respond. Moses has a deeper connection to his people than he understood at the moment. He was tempted to live out a simple life as a Midianite shepherd. We can't really blame him for that. He had already lived a dramatic life. His family and his people, however, called out to him. God reminded him of that call by speaking in the voice of his father.

I heard of an echo of this story when a forty-something man came to speak with me. He was in the process of building a successful career in public service. He was married with two young children. He had, however, very little contact with his parents. They had had a wonderful relationship through his college years and the beginning of his career. But much had changed because of his family and his brother. He felt his parents did not respect his wife. He felt his parents did not give his brother, who had serious special needs and could not live alone, the freedom to develop. He felt the way they cared for his brother was more about giving them something to do than about helping his brother thrive. He told me that when his parents were with his children, they spoke negatively of him and his wife and created more conflict. He told me the only way he could deal with this conflict was by totally cutting off contact with his parents and brother. It was the only way to protect his wife and children.

He came to me struggling to figure out what to do. I acknowledged his challenges were not easy. His values conflicted. He was tempted—for a very good reason—to set aside his relationship with his parents and focus on building a meaningful life with his wife and children. In some ways, it was breaking with his past to protect his future. But in coming to me, he was clearly indicating that the prospect of this total break was troubling him. He was at a tender point. I asked him to listen to his heart.

When we met again about a month later, he told me was in contact with his parents and brother. He still felt tension, of course, but he felt far more clear about his responsibility to both who he was and who he was becoming. I asked him what he heard when I suggested he listen to his heart. He told me he heard his father's comforting voice of love.

His father had also been in public service, and he cherished his father even as they experienced conflict. When he listened to his heart, he heard a voice that had been buried. That voice, he told me, helped him see what was not obvious before. He had to honor his parents and build a family and healthy relationship with his brother. He may not know every step he will have to take on that path, but his father's voice led him to see he had to take it. Moses did not know the exact steps that he would follow in returning to Egypt and leading his people to freedom. But after hearing his father's voice, he did know that was the path he had to take.

I AM YHVH

> *Moses said to God, "When I come to the Israelites and say to them, 'The God of your fathers has sent me to you,' and they ask me, 'What is His name?' what shall I say to them?"*
>
> *And God said to Moses, "Ehyeh-Asher-Ehyeh." He continued, "Thus shall you say to the Israelites, 'Ehyeh sent me to you.'"*
>
> *Exodus 3:13-14*

This commitment to a path without seeing every step along the way may seem confusing. Don't we look to God for answers? Why can't God reveal to us every step of our lives, every turn we must take? The answer to this mystery is found when we analyze God's name, which is revealed in this verse.

First, we have to realize that every translation of the Torah is, to a greater or lesser degree, an interpretation. The ancient Hebrews did not leave us a dictionary translating their language into others. Our translations are our best guess—informed by scholarship and teachers of the past—to capture what they meant. This is why many scholars of the Bible learn Hebrew. It's the only way we can hear the words of the Bible in all of their nuance and depth. Even then, however, certain words and phrases are hard to translate. This phrase is one of them.

The Hebrew words God speaks to Moses are *ehyeh asher ehyeh*. The standard translation has been "I am what I am." Some also say "I am who I am." But biblical grammar tells us something different. The word *ehyeh* means "I will be." It is the future tense. If we said, "I will be at work today," we would say "*Ehyeh b'osookah*." Thus, the more accurate translation would be "I will be what I will be," or "I will be who I will be." Why, then, do most translations use the present tense "I am"? Because they are influenced by the original Greek translation, the Septuagint. And the Septuagint reflects Greek philosophy, which is different than Jewish thought.

Greek philosophy understood God as a static being. Aristotle famously described the one God as the "unmoved Mover." Now the Greek gods were very different from the gods of the nations surrounding Israel, but the god of platonic philosophy within Greek thought led them to see the Israelite God as one existing apart and above all of humanity. God is permanent, never changing, without emotion. In other words, in Greek thought, there are two dimensions: the divine realm (the realm of perfection in Plato) and the human realm. The two are completely separate.

There are strands of Jewish thought that embrace this Greek perspective. But the Torah conveys a different philosophy. The God of the Torah is dynamic. God is not an unmoved mover. God is a moving, living being. God gets angry, as God did with Pharaoh and the Egyptians, as illustrated through the ten plagues sent on Egypt. And God even changes God's mind, as God did after Moses pleaded with God not to destroy the Israelites after the sin of the golden calf. The Israelite God is a God of relationship. More specifically, God lives and acts through history. God's dynamism is a sign of God's freedom.

For the Greek philosophers, God exists but then does nothing. God sets the world in motion and then steps back. The God of the Torah stays with the Israelites on their journey through the wilderness, leading them through thick and thin. Put simply, translating God's words to Moses as "I am what I am" teaches us that God is a God of being. Translating it as "I will be what I will be" teaches us that God is a God of becoming.

Why does this distinction matter? How does it help us in understanding the Israelite (and our own) path to salvation? Because a free and dynamic God is with us on our journey and gives us the freedom and creative power to act. Our paths are not preestablished and set in stone. As Jonathan Sacks puts it, "God is not an object. Neither are we.... We are the only beings thus far known to us who are capable of envisaging a future state of affairs that does not yet exist, and acting to bring it about. God, the Creator, by making us in His image, made us creative."[2] In other words, if God were static, we would be too. But like God, we have free will. This belief is essential to every other one. If we did not have free will, we would be like robots carrying on what is already programmed inside of us. We could not choose to follow the commandments. If we are Christian, we could not choose to believe the death and resurrection of Jesus. But we can choose to act. We can choose to believe. A dynamic God is essential to the entire Judeo-Christian life.

Our own development as individuals also depends on this freedom. We do not, however, experience it automatically. Like Moses, we have to stop, look, and listen. We need the humility to recognize the future is not always clear. Later in the Torah, Moses is described as the "most humble man on earth" (see Numbers 12:3). His humility allowed him to hear the voice of God.

Indeed, the Jewish sages teach that many people walked by the burning bush. God was inviting them to stop and look. They did not, however, notice. Only Moses stopped and noticed. This teaching was the sages' way of saying that many of us go through life without seeing the miracles around us. We sleepwalk through life. Moses, however, acted differently. He noticed and listened. That listening opened up the possibility for change. Moses listened to God, and God listened to the

Israelites' plea for freedom. God's invitation is waiting for each of us. And when we respond, God responds. When we listen, God listens.

ALL AS ONE AT MOUNT SINAI: REVELATION

Having journeyed from Rephidim,
they entered the wilderness of Sinai
and encamped in the wilderness. Israel
encamped there in front of the mountain,
and Moses went up to God.

Exodus 19:2-3

Moses listened at the burning bush. That was his seminal moment of revelation. The entire Jewish people experience revelation several chapters later, at the foot of Mount Sinai, beginning when they arrive at the mountain in Exodus 19. The translation of verse 2 misses one of the key insights captured in the Hebrew. As the Israelites stand at Mount Sinai, the Hebrew moves from the plural to the singular. They encamped (plural) in the wilderness, but Israel encamped (singular) in front of the mountain. The Jewish people are no longer a group of individuals. They are one people with one heart. This unity does not last. This verse is the only time in the Torah when the word used for the Jewish people is in the grammatical singular form. But in this moment lies an aspiration: the aspiration for wholeness, integrity, unity of all that is within and outside of us.

God's revelation of the Torah to the Israelites at Mount Sinai has similar theological significance for Jews that the resurrection of Christ has for Christians. The heavens and the earth touch. In the Gospels, Jesus resurrected is the bridge. In the Torah, the Torah itself is the bridge. This is the moment when God and humanity converge.

Even though it only lasts a moment, what does this moment mean for the development of the Jewish people? What can it teach each of us? It suggests that even amidst division and conflict—two features of political and social life around the world today—unity and understanding beckons. It is possible. The Jewish sages amplify this teaching with their interpretations of this verse and the context in which it takes place. They discern the characteristics and actions conducive to unity and survival.

The first characteristic is wonder. Experiences of wonder and awe draw us closer together. In Hebrew the word for wonder, fear, and awe is the same word. It is *yeirah*. One of the ways *yeirah* draws us closer together is by distorting our normal senses and feelings. These normal senses emphasize our separateness. We have *our* sense of smell or sense of sound. But at Mount Sinai, we read that the Israelites "heard the fire" and "saw the thunder." That is the Torah's way of saying that God upended the normal way we see the world, and with it the usual feeling of separation from others vanished. The people standing at the mountain felt it as one, as if they were one person with one heart.

Awe and wonder still bring us closer together. Abraham Joshua Heschel said that wonder keeps alive "the great fellowship of all beings."[3] It does so by reminding us of the reality of things and forces much larger than we are. Fear plays a role as well. Natural disasters, for example, bring people together because we would not survive without one another. Yet, even without life-threatening forces, awe and wonder open us up to others. They change our view of the world. Stanford University professor Jennifer Aaker has studied the power of awe and wonder. The author of *The Dragonfly Effect* said in an interview,

> When you feel awe, you are experiencing a positive emotion that feels vast and big, and as a result is capable of altering one's view of the world. Our studies focus on the effects of awe on how people may alter their sense of time—that is, the way they perceive and use time. We show that when people feel awe, they feel like they have more available time on their hands. And as a result, they are more willing to volunteer to help others, and spend time on others.[4]

Mount Sinai not only brought Moses and the people he was leading closer together. According to the Jewish sages, this momentary experience was felt by all Jews throughout history. In other words, they are saying that even the normal sense of time collapsed at the moment of revelation at Mount Sinai. Jews born three thousand years later were somehow at Mount Sinai at that moment. What are the Jewish sages trying to teach here? On the one hand, they are saying that God transcends time and space. God can speak to people across time if God wants to. In addition, however, the sages are saying that the truly meaningful experiences change our lives permanently. They last a moment, but they also last a lifetime because they shape the way we live and the legacy we leave. For the Jewish people, receiving the Torah at Mount Sinai changed their lives and the lives of their descendants forever. It is like the American Revolution and writing of the Constitution. It changed the lives of those who led it and signed it. And it also changed the lives of people living here 250 years later.

A third implication of this moment of revelation is that it establishes a baseline of equality among the Jewish people. It was not just the priests who experienced God's revelation. It was the entire people. This unity stands out from the experiences of other ancient Near Eastern cultures. Religious covenants usually bound gods and the king of a nation. The people were subordinate to the king. In the Torah, God makes the covenant with the entire Jewish people. Moses is the intermediary, not the king. The Torah echoes this message when God says all the Israelites are priests unto God. "All the earth is Mine," God says, "but you shall be to Me a kingdom of priests and a holy nation" (Exodus 19:5b-6).

On the surface, this teaching seems paradoxical. The Jewish people do have a priestly caste known as the Levites. They do have unique responsibilities and limitations. So why would God call every Israelite a priest? Because the Torah is available to all. Study and observance of the Torah lifts up every Israelite and brings them closer to God. There is a profound egalitarian thrust within Judaism. On one visit I made to Israel, a tour guide attributed this egalitarian thrust to the nature of the land.

The land of Israel has very few natural resources. Farming and agriculture are the only means of survival. Thus, every person depended on the rain, and rain does not discriminate between rich and poor, elite and commoner. In societies with natural resources—like the contemporary Middle East and oil—a small elite controlling the resources usually holds most of the power as well. That type of society never evolved in ancient Israel. The critical natural resource—water—could not be fully controlled. Farmers depended on each other to survive.

This explanation makes sense on a pragmatic level, but the Torah also suggests a spiritual component to this equality. Not only is the Torah available to all. Its ultimate vision is one where dignity and holiness is not a privilege of birth. A beautiful rabbinic teaching captures this truth. It also subtly incorporates the importance of the land in establishing Jewish values in the way my tour guide pointed out. Even though it is a bit mystical and seems to rely on supernatural miracles, which was rare in rabbinic teachings, it brims with values and vision:

Once Rav (a great second-century rabbi) came to a certain place where he had prayed and decreed a fast so that rain would fall. But no rain fell. Eventually someone else stepped forward in front of Rav and prayed, "You are the God who causes the wind to blow"—and then the wind blew!

Then the man prayed, "You are the God who causes the rain to fall"—and the rain fell.

Rav asked the man: "What is your occupation?" [i.e., what is your special virtue that causes God to answer your prayers]?

The man replied: "I am a teacher of young children. I teach Torah to the children of the poor as well as to the children of the rich. From those who cannot afford it, I take no payment. Besides, I have a fishpond, and I offer fish to any boy who refuses to study, so that he comes to study."

This simple story acknowledges the reality of the land. Life depends on rain. Not even the prayers of the greatest rabbi of the time have the power to cause rain. Yet, there is one man whose prayer is ultimately answered by God. It is the humble teacher of Torah: the one who teaches the young child, both poor and rich. The world of Torah is one open to all who seek its wisdom.

TABERNACLE

Creating a culture of universal dignity is, however, much harder than it sounds. It is not our natural human tendency. We tend to divide into tribes. Evolutionary biologists have demonstrated this truth in dozens of studies. The tribe was our way of surviving and protecting ourselves throughout history. Tribes usually included a "strongman" leader who kept order and discipline within the tribe. Jonah Goldberg calls this the "tribal desire for strongmen."[5] The "strongman" leader often consumed more power over time. History is replete with examples of tribes becoming nations with a tiny elite consisting of a "strongman" and his allies. Goldberg suggests human nature—both the desire for a leader and the corruptive tendencies of those in power—leads us down this path.

The Torah meant to change it. It is God's way of guiding us to transcend and escape the prison of natural tendencies. Whenever I teach my Torah study class, I always remind the students that the Torah does not forbid actions that human beings do not do. In other words, the Torah would not say "Do not steal" if people didn't steal. The Torah would not condemn adultery if people did not commit adultery! The Jewish sages teach that the Torah was "not given to angels." God recognizes our human frailty but seeks to lift us up through Torah.

One critical way God does this in Torah is the construction of the Tabernacle, the portable tent of meeting the Israelites carried with them in the Sinai wilderness. This project required the efforts of every Israelite. They built it together. This shared project brought them closer together. But it did not happen easily. Overcoming the divisive instinct of tribalism required time and effort. To put it in perspective, consider this comparison: God creates the world in three chapters, about forty-seven verses of Torah. It takes the Israelites over a dozen chapters and a thousand verses to create a portable ark. What explains this contrast?

The construction of the Tabernacle was not just about the construction of the Tabernacle. It was about forging a people out of a fractious group of former slaves. Just before the construction began, the Israelites had built an idolatrous Golden Calf. This act was the low point of the journey from Egypt to the Promised Land. It suggested the Israelites were not ready for God. They still yearned for the comforts of Egyptian idolatry and slavery. They had already complained numerous times to Moses about the uncertainty of their new life. In Egypt, they at least knew where their next meal was coming from. They felt uncertainty in their new way of life with an invisible God whose sole message was words conveyed through Moses. The Golden Calf represented a return to what was familiar.

God recognized that the only way they could forge a new identity and sense of purpose was through a shared project. God could not simply give them something. With God's guidance, they had to make it for themselves. Hence, the construction of the Tabernacle. And the construction is guided by two principles: voluntariness and diversity. The Torah begins its description of the project by saying that everyone gave "as their hearts so moved them." The result of this call for a free-will offering is a diversity of them. Each Israelite offers a different object or set of skills. One makes the curtain for the ark. Another gives the gold. Another chops the wood for the altar. It is through this act of creation—

this teamwork depending on the unique skills and cooperation of every Israelite—that the Tabernacle is constructed. And it is also through this act of teamwork that the Israelites become a nation. As Rabbi Jonathan Sacks put it,

> Moses was faced with the problem: How to turn a group of people—in his case, liberated slaves—into a nation with a collective identity? His answer was dazzling in its simplicity. You get them voluntarily to create something together.... The best way of making people feel "I belong" is to enlist them in a shared project so they can say, "I helped build this."[6]

My experience has taught me this is not only true in ancient times. It guides us today. When we took a synagogue trip to help rebuild homes in New Orleans after Hurricane Katrina, we grew closer together as a congregation. When we built a new building for the synagogue, we formed new friendships and ties to each other and to the congregation. When we do something together, we bond with and appreciate one another.

CONCLUSION

The Book of Exodus may be the most dramatic and eventful book of Torah. The Israelites grow from a clan of seventy people to a nation freed with dramatic plagues, miracles, and the revelation of the Torah at Mount Sinai.

One core purpose of these events is to transform the Israelites into God's people, chosen for a life of devotion in the Promised Land. Within that Promised Land will be a home for God on earth. By the time we get to the end of Exodus, the Israelites are still far from that land. According to biblical chronology, the revelation at Mount Sinai takes place seven weeks after the Exodus from Egypt. Thus, the Israelites have almost forty years more of wandering. But Exodus ends on a sublime note of unity.

First, Moses blesses the people. According to the rabbinic sages, Moses blessed them with these words: "May it be (God's) will that His Holy Presence (*Shechinah*) rest upon the work of your hands and let the delightfulness of the Lord our God be upon you." The language used to describe Moses's blessing of the people mirrors the language used to describe God's blessing of creation in Genesis chapter 1. The Tabernacle is a miniature version of God's creation, the physical home for God on earth.

Second, Exodus ends with an experience of the presence of God. Exodus begins with a sense of God's absence. The Israelites are enslaved. Their fate seems sealed. Slavery lasts for hundreds of years. Then God notices. God remembers the covenant made with Abraham. Then, at the end of Exodus, God's presence fills the Israelite camp. God appears as a cloud during the day and a fire at night. Having reached this point, the Torah turns now to the Book of Leviticus, which is dedicated to sustaining God's presence in the midst of the people through the service of the priests.

CHAPTER 4

LEVITICUS

I read a story recently about a minister who started a church plant in Michigan. The church succeeded magnificently, and the article was quite laudatory. One detail, however, caught my eye. The minister's first sermon series was all about the Book of Leviticus! He pointed out that many people read the Bible and reach "the Levitical wall." They stop reading the Bible because Leviticus raises so many troubling questions and can seem primitive and barbaric. I confess I once felt this way. But the more I study Leviticus, the more wisdom it reveals to me. It is like a Russian nesting doll. The further and further I go, the more rich layers emerge. We will unpack this wisdom, focusing in particular on the ways Leviticus teaches us the power of ritual to bring God's presence into our lives, and how rituals helped transform the people of Israel from ex-slaves into a liberated servant of God.

Before we examine particular verses, however, we need to know three guiding truths about Leviticus. First, it focuses mostly on the priests and their service in the Tabernacle. The Tabernacle was the portable tent of meeting the Israelite created in the wilderness, and it is the basis for the eventual construction of the Temple that stood in Jerusalem. Thus, the details surrounding the Tabernacle apply to the Temple as well.

The primary guardians and practitioners in the Tabernacle and Temple were the priests. The priests descend from the tribe of Levi, who was Jacob's third son. One of the names the Jewish sages give to Leviticus is *Torat Kohanim*, which means the Torah of the Priests. It may have even existed at some time as a separate priestly manual. This focus on the priests reflects a theological understanding of the role of the priests. The priests do not exist for themselves. They are a spiritual vanguard, leading the people to holiness. They are not inherently holier than other Israelites. Rather, through their behavior, they are to lead the entire Jewish people to holiness. Thus, when we analyze the lessons of the priestly rituals, we find guidance for the entire people. Their behavior set an example for all.

Second, the Book of Leviticus has two main sections. The first consists of chapters 1–16, which focuses on sacrifices and the role of the priests. They describe how to live in right theological standing with God. Then chapters 17–27 are about how to incorporate the theology into daily life. This section is known as the Holiness Code. It is here that we discover a model for using rituals to create a well-lived life.

Third, amidst some of the gory details of sacrifices and bodily fluids we see described in Leviticus, it helps to keep in mind the overarching theme: bringing God down to earth. The priestly and Temple rituals are so detailed because they aim to bring order out of chaos. Just as God created the world out of the *tohu* and *vohu*—the void and chaos—in Genesis 1, so the Israelites create order out of a broken world through the priestly ritual. The Tabernacle, and later the Temple, is a map of heaven. If you follow the right path, you arrive to commune with God. The Israelites need this path after four hundred years of slavery. The Book of Leviticus establishes a new sanctified way of life, so the entire people can ultimately live up to their charge of becoming a "kingdom of priests and a holy nation" (Exodus 19:6)."

SIN OFFERING

Part of the role of the Tabernacle and Temple rituals is to preserve shalom, peace, and *seder* (order among the Jewish people and between the Jewish people and God). The simplest way to preserve peace and order is to behave perfectly. It is to avoid sin. But human beings cannot be perfect. We sin. We err. In Hebrew, the word for sin is *chet*, which means "missing the mark." We are not evil because we sin. We are human.

Consequently, God prescribes a system by which we make amends for our sins. God provides a way to restore order. That is what we encounter in this verse. This type of sacrifice is known as a sin offering. It makes amends for us when we sin unintentionally.

Why do we need such a ritual? Isn't it fine, if we make a mistake, to simply say I'm sorry? Perhaps if we were angels, a simple apology would do. But rituals provide human beings with a kind of concreteness that helps comfort and heal us.

Consider an apology: We have all probably received apologies that we knew the other party did not truly mean. They said "I'm sorry" because someone told them to do so. Imagine how different than would feel if the person *did something* to make amends. If they spoke negatively about us to our boss, for example, what if they brought our boss into our office and apologized, and then helped us with another project? Part of the power of rituals is that they do not simply express ideas. They enact ideas, and actions speak louder than words.

Rituals also have a public dimension to them. For the ancient Israelites, sin was not always a private affair between one person and God. Sin affected the entire community. We see numerous examples of this idea in the Bible, such as when God punishes Joshua's army because one man stole booty from the enemy (Joshua 7). Thus, the public had an interest in a person making amends after a sin, and a prescribed ritual helped demonstrate that process within the community.

The minute details of the ritual also matter because they serve as a counterpoint to the reality of sin. In other words, we can never behave perfectly, but we can offer a perfect sacrifice. Taking care in our rituals leads us to take better care in our lives. Jesus echoes this argument in the parable of the talents when he describes a wealthy master telling two faithful servants, "You've been faithful over a little. I'll put you in charge of much" (Matthew 25:21, 23). In Leviticus, the care by which we offer a sacrifice is a model for the care by which we should aim to live. As Professor Arnold Eisen puts it,

> The discipline of ritual is designed to school us in the search for rightness and thereby to increase the chances that it will be achieved, that *we* will achieve it....What matters more is the model provided by ritual for the *perfection* we are meant to aim at in the rest of life, an ideal which it [the Torah] calls holiness.[1]

Ritual is not only, however, about achieving rightness. It is about achieving rightness in the *right* things. Rituals shape what we pay attention to. Consider the focus of our verse: it addresses unintentional sins. We might be tempted to think they are unimportant. I didn't know the speed limit. I didn't know I had to pay my taxes on this money. But as we might have learned when we got our driver's license: ignorance of the law is no excuse. Even unintentional mistakes matter. This ritual reminds us of that reality.

Knowing that we have a clear, concrete way to make things right when we err is also a deeply comforting truth. Imagine if a friend or a spouse could hold a grudge against us for every rude word we said or time we made a mistake. We would live in perpetual misery and frustration. Rituals offer us a way to navigate life with grace and perspective. We find ways to reconcile. We find ways to honor sacred moments. We find ways to mark the natural processes like aging. And, like the sin offering, we find ways to make things right when we have misstepped.

One common concern I hear when teaching Leviticus at both churches and synagogues is that so many minute and seemingly unimportant details are included throughout the text. If this Torah is meant to be God's eternal and timeless word, why did God sometimes make it sound like an Ikea instruction manual?

One reason is that the text is written in the language of biblical Hebrew. We do not know how the words sounded to the people living at the time. So while they may feel like tiny unimportant details to us, they may have been tremendously significant and meaningful details to those who first heard them.

But some larger ideas emerge from this focus on minute details. The first is that in the Torah and in ancient Jewish practice, aesthetics mattered. God wanted human beings to build and create sacred spaces in a precise way. Think about great artists and writers. They care about every detail. Because every detail helps create the desired feeling. God saw the Temple as the most sacred place on earth. Every detail mattered.

There is also a more subtle reason the Torah includes so many details, and it connects us back to the construction of the Tabernacle discussed in chapter 3. The construction of the Tabernacle was not only a building project. It was a process to generate unity and community among a fractured Jewish people. A shared set of tasks and goals brought the Israelites together after the disastrous construction of the Golden Calf.

In the Book of Leviticus, the priests undergo a similar process. As the Torah begins to outline the priests' responsibility, it focuses on precise daily rituals. These daily rituals help unify the priesthood, and thus bring them and the entire Jewish community closer to God. They unite by learning to follow precise details about how to sustain the Tabernacle.

If this idea sounds strange, consider the practices of the US army. When a new soldier begins service, one of the first things they do is learn how to make a bed. Celebrated Navy Admiral William H. McRaven even titled his best-selling book *Make Your Bed: Little Things That Can Change Your Life…And Maybe the World*. What does making your bed have to do with becoming a better sailor or person? It's a daily ritual. It is something you and every other sailor does. It helps establish the military culture of discipline and consistency.

In the Book of Leviticus, God is teaching the priests how to build a culture of holiness. Thus, the book starts with seemingly unimportant minute details about how they were to offer sacrifices.

PRIESTS

As we noted, Leviticus serves as a priestly manual. Priests are born into their status, but they must also undergo a process for serving in the Temple. Birth does not guarantee service. Chapter 8 describes the process by which the priests become sanctified for their duties.

The placement of the priest's consecration within Leviticus reveals part of its message. It comes in chapter 8, after the first seven chapters of Leviticus. Where have we seen the number seven before? The seven days of creation. The entire creation story revolves around the number seven. In the Hebrew text of this account, Genesis 1:1–2:3, the word *tov* "good" is used seven times. The word "God" appears thirty-five times; the word "earth" twenty-one, all multiples of seven. The entire passage of the creation story contains 469 (7 x 67) words.

So here we have the ordination of the priests taking place after the first seven chapters. A new creation—the Temple, God's home on earth—has been completed. Now we move to the people—the priests—who sustain this new creation. As we noted in chapter 3, the Temple itself is a complement to the creation of the world. It's God's home on earth. It's the eighth day, the first day of the new week.

The entire chapter echoes this idea of a new creation. Moses anoints Aaron and his sons seven times. Aaron and his sons have to wait for seven days outside of the Tabernacle to complete their ordination as priests. Even the language used to describe the unfolding of the ordination process echoes creation. Everything unfolds, "just as God commanded it."

What message is God sending by defining the priests' role as attendants of a new creation? God is holding out a vision of a sacred world. There is a tension between the world as it is and the world as it ought to be. Priests stand at the threshold between heaven and earth. They help the Israelites bridge that gap.

The primary way they do so is the offering of sacrifice. The Hebrew word for sacrifice—*korban*—expresses this very idea. It means sacrifice or offering, but it also means "closeness." The offering of animal sacrifices brought the Israelites closer to God. The priests' primary duty was to offer ritualized sacrifices on behalf the people. Much of the Book of Leviticus is dedicated to describing the types of sacrifices offered and how the priests were to do so.

Now, to our modern ear this practice raises many questions. Why sacrifices? Did God really need our animals and crops? Before we answer this question, we need to be clear about what sacrifices were not. They were not offerings of bribes to God. God would not overlook our sins if we offered the right sacrifices. The Hebrew prophets make that clear. Sacrifices were a tactile way of seeking forgiveness and reconciliation, but they were not a means of annulment or erasure.

Why, then, did the Torah implement a sacrificial system? Because God realized that we are willing to make sacrifices for what we love. We are willing to give from what is most valuable to us to demonstrate our love. Think of parents and children. Parents sacrifice time, money, emotional stress, and so much more for the sake of their children. Spouses sacrifice for one another. Citizens make sacrifices for their country.

For the ancient Israelites, their flocks and crops were their most valuable possession. To make an offering of these things to God exemplified their love and gratitude. God was as real to the ancient Israelites as the air we breathe is to us. To make an offering to God was to offer gratitude to the source of their lives and livelihood. Faith and sacrifice go hand in hand. Relationships and sacrifice go hand and hand. The *korban* brought God and Israel closer together.

According to the Jewish sages, sacrifices served another central purpose. They reminded the Israelites of the reality of terror, chaos, and death. Once again, the world as it presently exists is not the world as it ought to be. Holding an animal on the brink of death—and experiencing the smells and sounds and sights of a sacrifice—changes our perspective. We cling to life with more gratitude because we are aware of the reality of death. As Professor Arnold Eisen eloquently puts it,

> Leviticus reminds us of death repeatedly: not to make us morbid, or to have the prospect of the grave dominate our lives, but…to help us *contain* death inside a life of order, richness, and meaning—and to contain not only our individual deaths but the threat posed by all of the world's pointless suffering and terrible chaos to the sacred order that the Torah seeks to build.[2]

In other words, the offering of sacrifices helped the Israelites face up to what is hardest in life—the reality of suffering and of death. When we offer a sacrifice, we face that reality, but we also orient ourselves to a different world—to God's sacred abode, to the place of purity and holiness.

Now we cannot fully enter that world. In the Torah, no one fully bridges that gap between heaven and earth, not even Moses. The dangers of trying to bridge it too quickly are revealed in Leviticus 10, when Nadab and Abihu, two of Aaron's sons, are killed at the threshold of the Holy of Holies, the most sacred place in the Temple.

NADAB AND ABIHU

Now Aaron's sons Nadab and Abihu
each took his fire pan, put fire in it, and
laid incense on it; and they offered before
the LORD *alien fire, which He had not*
enjoined upon them. And fire came forth
from the LORD *and consumed them; thus*
they died at the instance of the LORD.
Leviticus 10:1-2

The brevity and message of these verses shock us. Every time I teach about it, students sigh and shake their heads, wondering what Nadab and Abihu did to warrant such a swift and dramatic death. The Torah itself does not answer this question. The only hint they give is that Nadab and Abihu offered an "alien fire."

The Jewish sages struggled with this story as well. They offer a variety of explanations, each trying to derive a lesson from Nadab and Abihu, which we will discuss below. But look first at the reactions of Aaron and Moses. Immediately after Nadab and Abihu are consumed by fire, Moses says to Aaron, "This is what the LORD meant when He said: 'Through those near to Me I show Myself holy, And gain glory before all the people.'" Aaron responds to Moses with silence. Poetically, the King James Bible translates the Hebrew for "Aaron was silent" to "Aaron held his peace."

Each of these reactions hints at broader character and theological issues. In effect, Moses is saying that as priests and sons of Aaron, Nadab and Abihu were especially close to God, and therefore had to abide by the highest standard of holiness. They failed to do so. Thus, God punished them publicly and absolutely.

Moses is fitting into his role as the unequivocating and sometimes aloof leader. We have seen him act this way before, both in Egypt and the wilderness. He is uncompromising and consistent. When people disobey, they face the consequences.

Aaron's reaction is more ambiguous. He may be in shock. He says nothing. The King James translation of his keeping "his peace" is itself an interpretation because it suggests Aaron was at peace. That may be true, but Aaron may also be in fear for his own life. Perhaps he did not know what Nadab and Abihu did wrong, and he fears that God may strike him down as well. Or perhaps he is angry at Moses for suggesting his sons deserved to die. He may be afraid, however, of challenging Moses in front of the people.

One year when I was teaching this text, a member of my study group argued that Aaron failed his children by remaining silent. He should have spoken up, my student said. It is almost inhuman not to say anything. Even if he ultimately has to accept God's judgment, Aaron could have at least said something. Job challenges God when his children die. Why didn't Aaron?

The answer may lie in what we know about Aaron's character. He is the ultimate peacemaker. The Jewish sages describe Aaron as a man who would see two people fighting, and then he would talk separately with each of them, saying the other one wants to make peace. Not only did he like making peace, he loved to be loved. He did not want to upset others. We saw evidence of this trait during the construction of the Golden Calf. Aaron didn't stop its construction. We can only imagine what Moses would have done in Aaron's place. He would have stood up and sternly shut down those building the calf, even if he had to risk his life to do so. Aaron did not. So perhaps Aaron simply does not want to vent his anger and confront God.

But sometimes our weaknesses are also our greatest strengths. Aaron may accept circumstances that Moses wouldn't, but Aaron is also able to accept God's judgment and even try to make peace when such judgment is difficult and tragic. Perhaps that quality is what makes him suited to be the high priest. The Torah foreshadows a broader biblical tension between priests and prophets. This tension is especially evident in the books of Kings and Samuel, but it originates in the difference between Moses and Aaron. Moses is a prophet. He hears God's word, and he communicates it to the people. He is uncompromising. When he sees wrong, he tries to right it. When he sees people disobeying, he inflicts the proper punishment. The prophet generally sees the world in black and white. What is right is right, and what is wrong is wrong, and there is no gray area.

Aaron is a priest. The priest mediates between God's word and the actions of the people. The priest does not have the luxury of simply proclaiming God's word. The priest must guide the people in responding to it. In other words, the priests tended to be more pragmatic and less radical than the prophets. They sought to preserve the status quo rather than dramatically change it. They were peacemakers rather than rabble-rousers.

The Torah makes clear that we need both types of leaders. Moses and Aaron succeed as a team. In fact, the Jewish sages make this case through their understanding of Moses's speech impediment. We read in Exodus 4 that Moses could not speak properly. Scholars are unsure of the exact meaning of the Hebrew. It simply says he was "heavy of tongue." Perhaps he had a lisp or stutter or some other impediment. As a result, Aaron served as Moses's mouthpiece. When Moses spoke with Pharaoh, it was Aaron speaking what Moses said to him.

In addition to its literal truth, the Jewish sages also find a broader insight in Aaron's ease and Moses's impediment. Aaron could easily relate to the people, whereas Moses was more aloof and distant. The people felt close to Aaron in a way they did not with Moses. We see evidence for this in the way the Torah describes each of their deaths. When Aaron dies, the Torah says, the people sobbed for thirty days. When Moses died, they simply mourned.

Thus, by making Aaron the high priest, God is highlighting the priests' role as intermediaries between God and the people. The priest needs to be close and relate to both. The type of person who can do that is one like Aaron, who embodies compromise, acceptance, and the pursuit of peace.

Even if we understand Aaron's response, we are still left bewildered by the incident itself. What did Nadab and Abihu do, and why did God punish them so swiftly and dramatically? The Torah does not give us a direct answer, but the Jewish sages suggested several possibilities. The simplest answer is that Nadab and Abihu made an unauthorized sacrifice. They sacrificed an animal or engaged in some sort of practice forbidden by God. The reason God punished them so dramatically is twofold. First, they are Aaron's sons, and thus are subject to the highest standards of holiness. We judge people's behavior differently based on what they do. For example, we look differently at a priest or a rabbi who engages in adultery than an accountant who does so. And we might look differently at a priest or rabbi who cheats on his taxes than an accountant who does. Yes, the acts are wrong in both cases, and yes, both priests and accountants are human and make mistakes. Yet, they have each chosen a certain way of life, as well as the privileges and consequences that follow. Any infraction by Aaron's sons warranted the strongest possible punishment.

A more subtle explanation is found when we look at this incident in the wider context of the emergence and significance of the priesthood and Temple. The

Israelites are undergoing a massive transition. They are moving from a state of slavery to one of freedom and service to an invisible, unitary God. The priesthood is a critical component in this transition. The priests are the spiritual vanguard, modeling for the people what is possible in following the Torah's way of life. When they fail in their task, they hurt someone other than themselves. They harm the entire people. Their role is utterly serious. Even a tiny mistake ripples outward. That is the price of being chosen. Thus, whatever Aaron's sons did, God had to swiftly contain the damage before it might harm the entire people.

This interpretation requires us to understand the nature of the Temple and Tabernacle. As God's residence on earth, it had an inherent holiness and fragility to it. Everything that happened in the Temple had to happen in precise and ritualized ways. Making a mistake was like touching an electric fence. You felt the shock immediately, and what happened was outside of your control. Aaron or the other priests could not simply say to God that Nadab and Abihu made a mistake. Rather, the punishment was automatic. In effect, by offering an unauthorized sacrifice, they touched an extremely high voltage electric fence.

Another way of looking at this incident is that it symbolized the difficulty of any major transition. Think of what happens when a country moves from dictatorship to democracy. Often, those transitions do not succeed, but even when they do, massive damage ensues throughout the process. These include war, terrorism, frequent violence. Egypt, for example, experienced the ten plagues as they transitioned from a state with Israelite slaves to one without them. As the Israelites transition into a free people, they will not escape the harsh reality that accompanies meaningful change. The deaths of Nadab and Abihu capture the pain of that transformation. The Israelite transition to a free people in the Promised Land will not be easy. Even those closest to God will feel the pain of this change.

A final interpretation looks at this incident from the perspective of the proper order of the priesthood. Making an offering at the Holy of Holies was a task reserved for the high priest. Only Aaron—or Aaron with his sons accompanying him—could make sacrifices there. But Nadab and Abihu could not accept the role of supporting actors. They wanted to make the sacrifices themselves. They had too much pride to accept their role and decided to offer their own sacrifices. But God established a particular order and sacrificial system, and by violating that order, Nadab and Abihu disrupted God's sacred place and mode of worship. Their punishment warned the Israelites not to violate the sacred order God established for them. That theme persists throughout the Book of Leviticus.

YOM KIPPUR

Aaron shall take the two he-goats and let them stand before the LORD at the entrance of the Tent of Meeting; and he shall place lots upon the two goats,

> *one marked for the* LORD *and the other*
> *marked for Azazel.*
>
> *Leviticus 16:7-8*

The focal point of the Israelites' sacred order is the inner sanctum of the Jerusalem Temple. It is known as the Holy of Holies, and it was the place where the high priest ascended on the Day of Atonement, the holiest day of the year. The Book of Leviticus has an entire chapter devoted to this day, which contains a description of a memorable ritual (Leviticus 16). Even though it is not practiced regularly today, it shaped our understanding of atonement and forgiveness. It defines the meaning of Yom Kippur. To understand the significance of the ritual, we will look at various interpretations and what they mean to us today.

What happened? The text tell us two goats were offered to God. One was offered in the customary way as a sacrifice overseen by the high priest. But the other was led into the wilderness for *Azazel* (Leviticus 16:21-22). What happened to the goat next in the wilderness is left unsaid. The Jewish sages offered various explanations of what happened there and why. Much of their interpretation centers on the meaning of the word *Azazel*.

Scholars do not know the meaning of the word *Azazel*. Some argue *Azazel* is a fallen angel. This is the depiction in the apocalyptic book of 1 Enoch, parts of which may have been written in the third century BCE. The goat sent to *Azazel* in this ritual, though, is not an offering to the fallen angel. Rather, it is a reminder to the Israelites of the consequences of disobedience. The goat will suffer in the rocky, dangerous wilderness, as *Azazel* did.

A more accepted interpretation sees *Azazel* not as referring to a separate being, but as the destination of the goat itself. *Azazel* refers to the rocky terrain of the wilderness, where God also dwells. The word *azaz* means "rugged," and *el* is another name for God. The *Azazel* might also refer to a rocky cliff where the goat would walk, and from which it would fall.

This notion of a cliff to which the goat would walk and ultimately fall to its death appears in the writings of several Jewish sages. The most comprehensive description and influential analysis was given by Maimonides, the greatest rabbi of the Middle Ages. Maimonides draws from earlier Jewish sages and suggests that the goat served as a scapegoat. The word *azel* can mean "to go away."

According to Maimonides, the high priest would symbolically transfer the sins of the people onto the scapegoat. The goat, as we will see below, was led into the wilderness and ultimately to its death. The death of the goat was a symbolic means of atonement for the people. The removing of the sins of the people reestablished their closeness with God. Drawing from the Mishnah—a first-century book of Jewish law— Maimonides describes the formal process whereby this atonement would happen. First, the high priest and his sons would say a blessing over the two goats. They were of identical size and weight. One goat, as we noted, was to be sacrificed in the conventional way to God, and the other one sent into the wilderness. The goats assigned for each task would be chosen based on lots.

The blessing said by the high priest served as a confession and a request for forgiveness on behalf of the priests, their families, and the entire people. Then the high priest would take a scarlet thread and wrap it around the horns of the goat sent into the wilderness. A portion of the scarlet thread would be tied to a rock near where the goat would walk off to its death. If the thread had already turned white by the time it was recovered, it was a sign that the people had been already been forgiven for their sins. This tradition derives from Isaiah 1:18: "Come, let us reach an understanding, —says the LORD. Be your sins like crimson, They can turn snow-white; Be they red as dyed wool, They can become like fleece." In any case, the thread would be displayed in Jerusalem. If it was not already white, the hope was that it would turn white over the course of the year, symbolizing God's forgiveness of the people.

The high priest selected a man to walk the goat through the wilderness. According to the sages, the tradition began with the high priest selecting another priest for the task. Over time, however, the responsibility fell to a non-Israelite. Perhaps the fear of not performing the duties properly and what the potential punishment would be deterred the high priest from appointing a member of the community. The man would lead the goat through ten different stations on a road through the wilderness between Jerusalem and a mountain in the Judean wilderness. Once a mountain ledge was in sight and they were on track for it, the goat's escort would leave and let the goat walk off alone. It would then fall to its death. The observer would walk over, report the death, and then bring the scarlet thread back to the priest to inspect.

Now this description of the process I just revealed does not come directly from the Torah. The Torah only includes the one short passage cited above (Leviticus 16:21-22). Rather, as we noted, it comes from the Talmud. The Talmud was composed and compiled decades after the scapegoat ritual had ended. Thus, we cannot be sure of the accuracy of their description. Yet, their understanding of the process teaches us about the meaning of reconciliation and forgiveness. God gave the Israelites a powerful and lasting way to mend relationships and draw closer to God, and the way Jews observe Yom Kippur today echoes many of the underlying ideas of the scapegoat ritual.[3] Whether we observe Yom Kippur or not, we can find wisdom and guidance in the truths behind it,

First, the scapegoat ritual provided a way of wiping the slate clean. The Jewish sages struggled with the concept of sin and reconciliation. In the same way we cannot "unsend" an email, or "unsay" something we said, we cannot "undo" a sin. What is done is done. Any apology may help mend a relationship, but it does not restore it. The scapegoat ritual gives us a way to start over. It's a spur to pause, consider, repent, and reflect. It changes our relationship to the past. The past no longer determines the future. Only God has the power to make this change possible, and it remains possible today. We may not send a goat to its death anymore, but we do practice rituals to wipe the slate clean. At my synagogue, we follow the practice of taking breadcrumbs and throwing them into a natural body of water. This act symbolically releases our sins. I often remind people who are throwing their sins away into the water with me that the word *kippur*, which means atonement, also implies a "covering up." We cover up and wipe away our sins. In this case, the water covers, wipes away, and flows away with our sins. These powerful symbols make abstract concepts concrete and meaningful.

Second, the scapegoat ritual draws from the power of spectacle. Imagine the feeling of the Israelites as a priest adorned in white walked one goat through the Temple, down its steps and into the wilderness. I imagine the tens of thousands of people—also all dressed in white, which is a custom on the Day of Atonement as a symbol of purity—parting, chanting, and watching the goat and its escort. The ritual dramatized the importance of forgiveness. The drama is not intended to entertain. It is intended to move us and transform us. The power of the moment is extended because we are experiencing it together. Watching the ritual from far away paled in comparison to experiencing it at the Temple.

Consider the way most meaningful spiritual moments happen in your life. Perhaps some of them happened while you were alone. Others probably emerged during a dramatic communal experience. At the synagogue where I grew up, one moment in the service always gave me tingles in the spine. The choir would proclaim the opening words of the Psalm

"Su Sh'orim," which means "Open the Gates," as the organ played, and the entire congregation stood. Simultaneously, the doors of the ark would open, and the rabbi would ascend and take hold of the Torah. The drama conveyed respect for the Torah and highlighted the seriousness of the message we were about to hear. It also echoed the experience of the Israelites at Mount Sinai. At Sinai, the gates of heaven opened, and God brought the words of the Torah down to Moses. Much of the priestly ritual we encounter in Leviticus gave the Israelites a concrete way to see and experience God's presence and message in the Temple.

GRACE AND FORGIVENESS

And this shall be to you a law for all
time: In the seventh month, on the tenth
day of the month, you shall practice
self-denial; and you shall do no manner
of work, neither the citizen nor the alien
who resides among you. For on this
day atonement shall be made for you to
cleanse you of all your sins; you shall be
clean before the LORD.

Leviticus 16:29-30

The scapegoat ritual also conveys a clue about the power of grace. This clue is carried forward in both the Gospels and in the Talmud. The clue is in verse 29 where God proclaims Yom Kippur and says it shall be a day where the Israelites "do no manner of work." Does this simply mean they were not to farm or do whatever work they did to make a livelihood on Yom Kippur? Perhaps, but the Hebrew word for work also means "worship." So is God also saying they should not worship on the Day of Atonement? That seems strange. Isn't the entire purpose of the Day of Atonement to worship God throughout the sacrifices of the priests, and thereby receive atonement? No. The Israelites do not earn atonement on Yom Kippur. They do not work to earn some reward because God does not "need" their sacrifices for sustenance or proof of faith. Rather, the sacrifices and the ritual are serving as witnesses for God's forgiveness. This belief emerges not only from our verse about doing no work. It also emerges from the Hebrew word for atonement, *kippur*. *Kippur* means "covering." It is not simply a physical covering. Think of the English idiom today, "I'm covered." It means "I'm taken care of." God takes care of us through an act of cleansing on Yom Kippur.

Now that does not mean Yom Kippur and the scapegoat ritual serve as a "get out of jail free" card. Jewish tradition does not take the idea of grace to a radical extreme and argue that it does not matter what one does, and God forgives everything automatically. The best way to understand this truth is to see the difference between "atonement" and "appeasement." Appeasement suggests we are offering something to God to appease God, and thereby achieve forgiveness and a restoration of our closeness to God. We offer. God accepts. Atonement implies just what the word says: "At-one-ment." We are restoring a closeness to God. That is why Israelites offered the sacrifices and symbolically transferred their sins to a goat sent into the wilderness. Those concrete actions symbolized a transformation in themselves to restore a sense of closeness to God. Sin had come between the people and God. God wipes away that barrier with forgiveness. The Israelites removed the barrier within themselves through the rituals of Yom Kippur. They became "at one" with the one God of the universe. God did not need it. But they did.

The Jewish sages sought to ensure that the people did not believe Yom Kippur served as a "get of out jail free" card with another teaching about the meaning of atonement. In the Talmud they suggest that "For transgressions between a person and God, Yom Kippur atones; however, for transgressions between a person and another, Yom Kippur does not atone until he appeases the other person" (Mishnah Yoma 8.9). In other words, God does not forgive us on Yom Kippur for stealing from another person *unless* we have sought forgiveness from that person. According to the Torah, on Yom Kippur, God forgives the times when we did not follow proper ritual or observe the holy days in the prescribed fashion. But God does not wipe the slate clean for ways we hurt others if we have not sought to reconcile with them. This teaching emerges out of the belief that every human being is created in the image of God. Therefore, unless we have sought to reconcile with a human being where we have sinned, we still experience a barrier between us and God. Seeking reconciliation requires remorse and attempts at restitution. We cannot ask for forgiveness without examining and seeking to change ourselves. If we do feel remorse and attempt restitution, and the other party still does not accept our request for forgiveness, then, according to Jewish tradition, we must ask them up to three times. If they still refuse, God serves as a proxy and forgives on that person's behalf.

When I have taught this rabbinic idea at churches, some have suggested that it feels too legalistic. Why must we go through a process to achieve forgiveness if God is filled with grace? The answer is twofold. First, part of the purpose of God's teaching in the Torah is to guide the Israelites in establishing a society and a nation. They are journeying through the wilderness to the Promised Land where they will build a civilization as God's chosen people. In other words, God's teachings are intended not just for the individual, but for the community as a whole. If lying and cheating and stealing and murder could simply be wiped away on the Day of Atonement, then a society could not function. There is no separation in the Torah between religious and civil law, as there is today. Everything existed under religion. God's laws not only speak to our personal relationship to God but establish the ways in which the community together can function and relate to God. Thus, God provides a process by which human beings can reconcile.

Second, as we noted earlier, the rituals do not exist to satisfy God. To think they are only for God is a way of avoiding their significance. It is like saying when we apologize to someone that we're sorry for the way our actions made *them* feel. An apology is not about the other person. It's about changing ourselves. The same is true with the rituals of Yom Kippur. They shape us. Rabbi Alan Lew wrote a book about Yom Kippur in which he argues that our daily lives do not prepare us for the spiritual transformation God opens up for us on the Day of Atonement.[4] Without it we would collapse. We would get caught up in the daily grudges and limited perspective of life. Over time we would lose touch with our relationship with God and the potential in our relationships with one another. Rabbi Lew compares life without the Day of Atonement to the Maginot Line set up in France in World War II. The line was well fortified, but the Germans invaded France from a different direction. Rabbi Lew says that in the same way, life comes at us from a different direction than we expect. The Day of Atonement helps us deal with the unexpected yet ever-present reality of chaos and sin. The Israelites in the Bible strengthened themselves when they practiced the rituals of the Day of Atonement. As the day ended, a sacred order was restored, both in their lives and in God's relationship with the community.

LOVE YOUR NEIGHBOR AS YOURSELF

God's sacred order does not, however, depend only on ritual. It also rests on a principle described today as the Golden Rule. Leviticus 19 contains this seminal verse: "Love your fellow [neighbor] as yourself." The

Jewish sages affirmed it as a core teaching, but they also reformulated it by teaching, "What is hateful to you, do not do unto another." This reformulation, as we will see below, helps make us more capable of living by the Golden Rule. Before we examine its various interpretations and applications, however, let us consider its context.

It comes amidst a series of ritual and agricultural laws like: do not reap your harvest to the corners of your field (19:9) and do not wear clothing woven of two kinds of material (19:19). In other words, it seems out of place. If you are giving a speech, you usually build up to make your most important point. Point number 1 builds up to point number 2, which culminates in point number 3. But here it seems like we go from point number 5 to point number 1 to point number 9 in terms of significance. Loving your neighbor as yourself seems like the most significant verse, and it should be the culmination of the Torah, rather than a phrase stuck at the end of a verse in the middle.

Its placement reflects a core truth of the Torah and ancient Judaism. There is no separation between "religious" and "secular." In Judaism, everything we do in our lives is part of our relationship with God. The covenant between God and Israel is holistic and all-encompassing. God cares as much about what we do at the kitchen table as what we do at work or in our bedrooms. God cares about politics and about family life. God cares as much about how we pray as how we treat other human beings. In other words, there are no levels of significance in evaluating the different laws of the Torah. They all matter equally.

This idea may seem strange to us. How can the mixing of two types of material in one's clothing matter as much as how we treat one another? The answer, according to traditional Jewish theologians, is that the entire Torah is God's word. It is not our task to distinguish between its commandments. We trust that all of them come from God, and we do not know what is in God's mind or what actions are truly important to God. All we have is our human understanding, but God's perspective is beyond our comprehension. Thus, we trust in God's word as it has been revealed to us.

While I do not subscribe fully to this theology, I do think it demonstrates humility. We do not know all the reasons and origins for the laws of the Torah, but we do not automatically replace God's judgment with our own. Sometimes laws exist for reasons we can't conceive, and often what we think of as unimportant is much more significant than we could have imagined. In 1952, author Ray Bradbury wrote a short story titled "A Sound of Thunder" about this idea. His story was a narrative portrayal of what is popularly known as the "butterfly effect." The story tells of a group of hunters from the year 2055 who use a time machine to go back to a time when dinosaurs roamed the earth. They are permitted only to hunt preselected animals that were going to die anyway, and they promise not to do any action—however small—that might alter the future.

In the middle of their hunt, one of the men named Eckels gets scared and runs off the preselected path.

He returns shortly, and everything still goes as planned. When they arrive back, however, recent election results have changed. Spelling on signage is different. They soon discover a dead butterfly on the sole of Eckels's shoe. That small act changed the course of history. Who knew what effect stepping on a butterfly would have? Who knows why certain laws exist? Sometimes the traditions of the past have wisdom we do not understand.

Most of us do understand, however, the ethical importance of the message of the Golden Rule: love your neighbor as yourself. Psychologists might say that it speaks to a part of human nature that craves reciprocity. That is, psychologists have done extensive research uncovering a natural instinct to do something for someone who does something for us. For example, if someone invites us to their home for dinner, we feel inclined to invite them to ours. Leviticus 19 elevates this natural instinct to a more comprehensive plane: we treat others as we want to be treated. If we would like others to be honest with us, we speak and act honestly toward them. If we hope others are kind to us, we need to act kindly toward them.

The Jewish sages understand that the Golden Rule functions as a way of building civilization and society. A commitment to it is necessary to create basic social trust that allows people to cooperate and build things that no one person could build alone. The Jewish sages did question, however, how realistic it is to expect us to apply the Golden Rule to everyone in the world. Consider, for instance, people who want to immigrate to the United States. The Golden Rule suggests we should allow them to do so, since we would want to be treated the same. But what if three billion people wanted to immigrate? Allowing such a large number to immigrate to the United States would lead to negative consequences external to the simple idea of doing unto others as we would want them to do unto us. So the principle that applies when considering individuals doesn't always translate smoothly to society-wide matters.

In addition, the Golden Rule suffers from another problem. What about people who do not want to be treated in the way we are treated? Think about suicide bombers who want to murder themselves and others for what they think of as a higher cause? Do they share our desires? Welcoming a suicide bomber into our home seems to be the height of naivete rather than ethics.

The Jewish sages struggled to make sense of what God meant with the Golden Rule by probing beneath its seemingly simple surface. First, they looked at two of its key words. The first is "fellow" or as it's often translated, "neighbor." Who is our neighbor? When we think of the word today, we think of physical proximity. Our neighbor lives next door to us, or perhaps in the same block or city. Clearly, however, the word *neighbor* in this context is talking about something more than that. Is the word *neighbor* another way of saying every other human being? Perhaps, but then why did the Torah not use the Hebrew phrase *kol adam*, which means "every human being"? That would have clarified the issue. The Jewish sages debate this issue and end up with several opinions. One rabbi says the word *neighbor* refers to other Israelites, in which case the word *fellow* is probably a better translation. In other words, we treat our kinsmen as we would like to be treated. But the matter does not apply to people from other groups.

Another sage, however, Rabbi Akiba, said our neighbor is every other human being because every human being is created in the image of God. He sees Leviticus 19:18 as a recognition of a basic human equality. What Akiba does, though, is examine the meaning of the second key word *love*. He draws from the teachings of his teacher, Rabbi Hillel. Hillel taught that we cannot be commanded to have a particular feeling. Thus, to *love* your neighbor as yourself was not about feeling a certain way toward a neighbor. It is about action. But then Hillel acknowledges the impossible standard of acting toward every person in the same way we would want them to act toward us. He suggests that only God can love so broadly. Loving our neighbor as ourselves is an ideal to which we may strive, but which we cannot reach as human beings. Hillel says that one of the ways we can move closer to that ideal is to not do unto our neighbor what we would not want done unto ourselves.

There is another dimension to Hillel's teaching relevant to our understanding of Torah. Hillel's words come from the Talmud amid a dialogue with a prospective convert to Judaism. This convert asks Hillel to summarize the entire Torah while standing on one foot. This prospective convert had asked another rabbi to do the same thing, and that rabbi brushed him off. Hillel, however, answers him with his reformulation of the Golden Rule, "What is hateful to you do not do unto another." He then adds, "All the rest is commentary. Now go and study." Thus, Hillel's golden rule is an answer to the request to *summarize the entire Torah*. His answer gives us a glimpse into the way the Jewish sages understood the purpose of Torah. It is to refine our human character. It is to transform us into better human beings. Our good deeds bring us closer to God. The Torah is not so much about teaching us what to believe as it is about teaching us how to live.

CONCLUSION

Leviticus is not an easy book to read or study. It speaks of blood, sacrifice, purity. It centers around an ancient structure that no longer exists as it once did. For many readers Leviticus's words can seem distant, even alienating. Yet, it may also be the most modern and relevant book because it teaches that faith is lived in the here and now. Faith is something we do. In Leviticus, the priests created a sacred space for God. That sacred space served as a model of what the world could be. The entire Torah is a guide for creating a sacred space for God on earth. It starts in the Temple and radiates outward.

CHAPTER 5

NUMBERS

The English name for the fourth book of the Torah—Numbers—does not have any thematic or linguistic connection to its Hebrew name, *bamidbar*, which means "in the wilderness." The English name derives from the several censuses conducted in the Book of Numbers. The first census appears in our opening chapter. The ostensible purpose of the census is to determine the number of potential soldiers. That's why it focuses on males at or above the age of twenty and excludes the priests. Its deeper purpose, however, is to remind us of the sanctity of every individual. This theme of the sanctity and significance of the individual recurs throughout Numbers.

The census also presages another key theme: the journey through the wilderness. That theme is hinted at in the Hebrew name of the book, "in the wilderness." Numbers depicts for us the challenges the Israelites face in their journey. It models for us a journey of faith. We witness both a lack of trust in God's promise and a reaffirmation of a commitment to that promise. We see the loss of key leaders and the emergence of new ones.

We see trials and triumph, often in the same chapter, culminating in the Israelites' arrival at the very edge of the wilderness, looking into the Promised land.

NUMBERS

Take a census of the whole Israelite community by the clans of its ancestral houses, listing the names, every male, head by head.

Numbers 1:2

None of us want to feel like a number. A number is impersonal. It is an objective reference point. Numbers have been used to dehumanize people: to make them feel and appear to be an object, not a subject. I think of prisoners of Nazi concentration camps who had numbers tattooed on their arms. To the Nazis, they were a number, not a human being. Some numbers were eliminated by murder. Others served to perform work for the German army. The numbers replaced the people.

For several Holocaust survivors I have spoken to, however, the numbers tattooed on their arm today serve a different purpose. The numbers remind them that they are, in fact, more than a number. It tells them they survived the dehumanization and murder all around them so they could share their unique experience and message with the world.

That is one of the ways the rabbis interpret the census that opens the Book of Numbers. The Israelites count individuals because every individual counts. The impetus for the rabbis' interpretation is the phrase used to describe the process of taking a census. The Hebrew translated in verse 2 as "take a census" is more literally translated as "raise the head." Moses is to "raise the head" of the Israelites. In other words, the Israelites raise their heads to be counted. Why does the Torah use this strange phrasing? Biblical Hebrew has several words meaning "to count," including *limnot*, *lispor*, *lifkod*, and *lachshov*. Why use this strange phrasing of raising the head? Because it contrasts the Jewish understanding of God and the individual with the Egyptian perspective.

Think of the Egypt of the pharaohs. To Pharaoh, the Israelites were workers who served the purpose of building the pyramids and the cities of Ramses and Pithom. They were means to an end, not ends in themselves. We see that same perspective in the biblical story of the construction of the Tower of Babel. The people of the earth decide to build a tower from earth into heaven. God disrupts their plans, deciding to confuse their languages so they could not speak with and understand one another. The Jewish sages suggest that God did so because the builders had no regard for human life. If a worker fell while he was adding a brick to the tower, the builders didn't care. Human workers were easily replaceable. But if a brick fell, they cried, because bricks took time and effort to create. God disrupted their plans because they rejected God in the form of the individual.

The Torah suggests that every individual has infinite value because every person is created in the image of God. This is not a value held in the worldview. Think of the tens of millions of people involuntarily drafted into armies and building projects in Stalinist Russia or Mao's China. In such dictatorships and cultures, people become just numbers. The Torah establishes a different understanding. None of us can be substituted for or by another. The Jewish sages reinforce this concept using a metaphor from the marketplace. They say, "something which is counted, sold individually rather than by weight, can never be nullified even if mixed in a thousand or a million others" (Beitzah 3b). In other words, if a food is sold individually, we pay for it and enjoy it separately from others. The Torah probably would not have permitted happy meals or buffets! The sages are using food as a metaphor for the uniqueness of the individual. We are separate and whole. This understanding of the uniqueness of the individual is a result of our understanding of God. The one God of the universe is singular and unique. Thus, every individual created in God's image is unique. Science bears this out. Even genetically identical twins do not necessarily share the exact same physical characteristics or personality.

There is another dimension to the act of counting that makes it such a powerful teaching to begin the Book of Numbers. The Israelites are at a vulnerable time. First, they need to raise their heads. They are unique individuals. At the same time, as we read in the Book of Genesis, it is not good for man to be alone. We are individuals who become whole in relationship.

In the Torah, the relationships binding us not only include family. They encompass the tribe to which we belong. Today the word *tribe* can suggest exclusivity and division. That is not their function in the Torah. In the Torah the tribe is the Israelites' extended family. Each tribe began with one of the twelve sons of the patriarch Jacob. The tribe provided each Israelite an identity beyond their immediate family. Each tribe tended to have unique skills and responsibilities as well. The Levites served as the priests. The tribe of Dan tended to serve as judges. The tribe of Gad tended to serve as warriors and military leaders, and so forth. The tribe was the community within the larger people. Each tribe provided a path by which its individual members could walk. And, as we will see, the ways the Torah arranges the tribes provides a blueprint for the ways different groups can coexist in peace and harmony. In other words, the arrangement of the tribes is an early example of the ideal of e pluribus unum, out of the many, one. In a world of increasing tribal division, the Torah's model can provide important guidance.

CARRYING THE BANNER

The Israelites shall camp each with his standard, under the banners of their ancestral house; they shall camp around the Tent of Meeting at a distance.

Numbers 2:2

The picture here is stunning. An array of people holding banners surrounding the Tabernacle. God's people marching through the desert. Yet, the image was not one designed simply to impress. The Jewish sages make it clear that the Torah seeks to convey the essence of each tribe and their critical role as part of the mosaic of the Jewish people. As they write, "Reuben's flag was red and had mandrakes painted on it; Simon's was green and had Shechem (a city) painted on it; Judah's was blue and had a lion painted on it" (Numbers Rabbah, 2). The flags symbolized each tribe's uniqueness. And together they formed a diverse whole.

The Jewish sages teach that not only was the array of flags themselves significant, but that the arrangement and order of the tribes' flags was also essential and revealing. They are arranged very specifically, with each tribe having its place around the Tabernacle. (There are technically thirteen tribes including the priestly Levites, though they did not carry a flag.) The Levites stood next to the Tabernacle and encircled it. They were responsible for assuring it remained sanctified. Then the twelve tribes encircled the Levites, marching in four groups with three tribes in each one. They are like parts of a machine. They are arranged in a particular order so they can march and act effectively together. Some sages suggest that when they stood in the proper order, the twelve points encircling the tabernacle created a Star of David. Other sages suggest that the tribal order ensured that tribes in conflict with each other did not stand next to each other. In other words, God did not arrange the tribes haphazardly. The subtle details of the arrangement remind us that bringing different groups together is not always easy. It takes empathy and wisdom.

The Jewish sages then creatively extend the arrangement of the tribes around the Tabernacle to teach us about the connection between different generations over time. Every generation of the Jewish people, they write, has its own character and identity. Each carries its own banner, defined by the challenges and possibilities of the times. One generation joins another and each sees itself as a continuation and an advancement of God's underlying mission for the Jewish people. The Tabernacle, and then the Jerusalem Temple, symbolize their shared goal.

We can learn from this teaching whether we are Jewish or not, because each of us comes from somewhere and is going toward some place. We are links in a chain of a family, a nation, a community. This understanding does not diminish our own uniqueness. Indeed, the Israelites are identified as individuals before they are identified as part of a tribe. Rather, we add our voice to the various stories and communities of which we are a part. Another metaphor the Jewish sages use is that each person is like a letter in a Torah scroll. If one letter is missing, a word doesn't make sense. If the word doesn't make sense, the sentence doesn't make sense. If a sentence doesn't make sense, the paragraph is incomplete. If the paragraph is incomplete, the chapter and the book is incomplete. In other words, the world is incomplete without every person. The sages draw all of this from the arrangement of the tribes around the Tabernacle in our Torah verse.

THE PRIESTLY BLESSING

Thus shall you bless the people of Israel.
Say to them:

The LORD *bless you and protect you!*
The LORD *deal kindly and graciously*
with you!
The LORD *bestow His favor upon you*
and grant you peace!

(Numbers 6:23-26)

These are among the most well-known verses of the Torah. They constitute the oldest known blessing within Judaism. Archaeologists have concluded that it is at least 2,600 years old, and likely older than that. In 1979, two small silver scrolls were found in a dig in the Old City of Jerusalem with portions of this priestly blessing inscribed on them. The scrolls can reliably be dated to the end of the First Temple Period, around 600 BCE. The blessing has been recited regularly for most, and likely all, of that time.

Part of the power the blessing has comes in its structure. There are three words in the first line, five words in the second, and seven in the third. Furthermore, there are fifteen consonants in the first line, twenty in the second, and twenty-five in the third.[1] The buildup suggests an overflowing and abundance of God's blessing. But it conveys more than that. The words are not only beautiful, they reflect a theological understanding of God's role in the world and the way we live and share God's blessings.

The first clue to its broader meaning lies in the subject. The priests say "May God bless you and keep you." The priests themselves are not the source of the blessing. God is. The proper name of God is repeated in each line of the blessing. Acknowledging God as the source of blessing helps ensure that priests do not mistake themselves for God. We all know of times when religious leaders took their own sense of self too far and used their influence and power to exploit others. The most ancient blessing in Judaism reminds us of their proper role.

It is not only the priests who serve as God's conduits. We all do. Bestowing blessings is not something reserved for the priests. Every person can. And when we bless each other, we do so as conduits rather than originators. As Rabbi Shai Held puts it "We are not sources but channels of blessing. We do not create the goodness we bestow but rather pass it on.... God—and not we—is the source of blessing, and in giving we pass along a bounty ultimately not ours."[2]

The Jewish sages also ask what the Torah means when it says "may God bless you." With what will God bless us? What do you think when you hear those words? Are they conveying our hopes for material prosperity? for happiness? for protection from harm? Yes, the rabbis suggest. All of the above. But they also explore the language of the blessing to suggest a more subtle understanding. The priests say, may God bless *you* and protect *you*. The hope is that each person receive blessings appropriate to him or her. May the Torah scholar receive greater insight and understanding, and may the merchant receive more orders and profit. As we noted earlier, the Torah cherishes the uniqueness of every individual, and each individual needs different kinds of blessings.

From this understanding of blessings flows the sages' insight into the next part of the verse, "May God *protect* you." Our initial interpretation might be that the priests are invoking God's protection against physical danger. Given that the Israelites are wandering through the wilderness, this view makes sense. Yet, the sages connect the meaning of "protect" with "bless" and suggest we are asking God to "protect us lest the very blessing we receive turn into a stumbling block." In other words, if we are blessed with wealth, we may become greedy. We may turn our hearts away from others. We may feel anxious that we never have enough. Or if we are blessed with great knowledge and wisdom, we may lose our humility. We can become arrogant and confuse our beliefs with God's absolute truth. In other words, our limited human understanding of God can become an idol.

Think, for example, about Jews or Christians two hundred years ago who believed slavery was ordained by God. Or think about extremists today who justify murder in the name of defeating infidels. Without humility, faith can legitimate cruelty in the name of kindness. We need God's protection from the way we can abuse and manipulate the truths God gave us.

One of the twentieth century's most admired Jewish sages, Abraham Joshua Heschel, captured this idea beautifully when he wrote, "There has, indeed, been so much pious abuse that the Bible is often in need of being saved from the hands of its admirers."[3] I like to think that we are asking God for the blessings of remaining faithful to what God asks us to do, and to protect us from the arrogance of believing we always know the exact answer for what God asks us to do. We are asking God to not allow us to turn our blessings into curses.

The second line of line of the blessing is a bit more mysterious. What does the Torah mean when we ask God to let God's face shine upon us? Does God have a face? Does something emanate from God's face? Are we asking to look like Moses did when he came down from Mount Sinai with a halo hovering behind his head? The answer lies in the ambiguity of the Hebrew. Rather than translate the second verse as "May God's face shine upon you," we can translate it as "May the light of God's face shine out from your face." In other words, may the people you encounter find traces of God's presence on your face. May your actions and your words lead people to God. One of my rabbinic mentors, Harold Schulweis, used to talk about God as a verb. God's presence becomes evident when we act in godly ways. We cannot fully know God the noun, Schulweis taught, but we know godly behaviors when we see them. When the priests call upon God's light to shine down upon us, they are asking God to help us embody God's teachings. Rarely do we prove the existence of God with logic or science. We illustrate God's reality by the way we live.

And the second half of this verse defines what it means to live in godly ways. We show *chen*, or grace. Sometimes it seems we have minimized the meaning of grace. We think it refers to good manners or refers only to the blessing we might say before meals. But grace is a profoundly religious trait. It refers to a perspective and set of behaviors that combine tenderness with conviction. The best example is the biblical patriarch Abraham. When the flocks and servants of Abraham and his nephew Lot begin fighting with each, they decide they need to separate. Abraham trusts that God will lead him to the right place, to the Promised Land. Therefore, Abraham says to Lot, "Let there be no conflict between us. Choose which way you want to go, and I will go the other." Abraham wishes his nephew well and lets him decide where to go. When Lot and his family are endangered several chapters later, Abraham immediately responds and goes to rescue him. Grace is kindness, but it is also much more. It is living mindful of the constant presence of God. This faith endows one's life with grace. As Rabbi Norman Lamm put it in describing Abraham: "For Abraham… this marshalling of all the forces of his life, even the mutually contradictory ones, means that he makes every aspect of his personality available to God, that he focuses all his power towards a higher goal, that all his existence is informed with a sense of transcendent purpose."[4] That is to live with grace.

This understanding may surprise us who tend to think of grace as a divine quality that God shows toward human beings. By God's grace we are forgiven or rewarded, for example. That understanding of grace exists within Judaism, but the sages tended to place more emphasis on our living with grace rather than receiving it from God. Indeed, God blesses us with the capacity to live with grace, and the priests invoke this capacity in our blessing.

The final verse asks God for shalom, peace. Peace is so critical that its placement at the end of the verse disrupts the rhythm of the blessing. Whereas the previous verses had ended with a *cha* sound, meaning "to you," the last verse ends with the consonant closed "m" sound of shalom. Shalom means peace, but it means much more than peace as the absence of conflict. It comes from the Hebrew word for "completeness," *shalem*, which also means "fullness" and "integrity." Peace is a state of being as much as a vision of the state of the world.

In the context of our verse, the Torah seems to be focusing on this state of being. The priest is asking God to give *us* peace. The first part of the verse hints at the way the God goes about doing so. We ask God to "lift up the divine face" upon us. In other words, we ask God to *notice* us. We are acknowledging the divine love that notices us as an individual. God's love penetrates the world, and the priests serve to invoke and focus it. That is a critical part of their task. The Talmud teaches that the priests would recite a particular blessing before they blessed people where they would say, "Blessed are You, Eternal God, Ruler of the Universe, Who has sanctified us with the sanctity of Aaron and commanded us to bless His people Israel with love." This blessing is the only one recited before performing one of God's commandments where we specifically ask to perform it in *love*. And it is also the only blessing where the priests ask to be sanctified with the *sanctity of Aaron* rather than the sanctity of God's commandments. What explains these unique features? I think it is the imperative of the priests—and anyone who seeks to bless others—to embody love. In this case, it is the love of human beings for one another. We will talk about love between God and human beings in the next chapter, when we look at the verse "And you shall love the LORD your God with all your heart and with all your soul and with all your might" (Deuteronomy 6:5). When it comes to the priests, however, their responsibility is to love the people. That was the defining character trait of Aaron, the high priest. One twentieth-century rabbi said, "The holiness of Aaron flowed from his love."

According to the Jewish sages, to love the people is to be attuned to their needs. It is to know them as unique individuals. The model for this is when Jacob blesses his sons before his death. He offers each of them a blessing unique to their character. In the case of the priests blessing the Israelites in the wilderness, the people needed to be reassured of God's presence. They shared that need. That is one of the reasons the priests turned toward the people when they blessed them. The priests could have looked up toward the heavens—or even to the ark, where God's presence was believed to dwell—as they blessed the people. But they looked *toward* the people because they were reassuring the people that they were worthy of—that they could receive—God's blessing.

This may sound strange to us, but the Israelites needed such reassurance. Given their history, why would the people feel capable of receiving God's blessing? They were traumatized by four hundred years in Egypt. Many still saw themselves as slaves. They complained about the uncertainty of the wilderness and yearned for a return to the predictability and comforts of Egypt. They embodied a state of being described by psychologist Martin Seligman as learned helplessness. That is an illness where conditions like imprisonment and abuse have programmed people's minds to accept these conditions as permanent. In such a condition, people struggle to accept the blessings and kindness of others. They see themselves as worthless and deserving of their ill fate. The priests' words seek to penetrate through that fog of unworthiness. By turning toward the people, they lift them up.

This understanding of blessing reinforces our theme of the Book of Numbers. It reflects the challenges and opportunities of the journey through the wilderness toward the Promised Land. It is a journey each of us experiences even though we live thousands of years later. Like the Israelites, we derive strength from the blessings of others. Think about moments in your life when the kind words or gestures of another has lifted you up. Perhaps those words were exactly what you needed to hear at that time. They were like a taste of water when you felt you were dying of thirst. That is the purpose of a blessing. Indeed, the Hebrew word for blessing is *bracha*. The same Hebrew letters—with a change of one vowel—form the Hebrew word for "pool of water." The same letters also form the Hebrew word for "bent knee." This connection is no accident. Imagine you are in the desert, and you come across a pool of water. You bend down on your knees and drink fully. The water gives you life. It restores you. That is what a blessing can do as well.

In Jewish tradition, priests and rabbis are not the only source of blessing. They are a model for the way we can bless one another. We bless one another through physical gestures like a gentle touch or hug. But what Jewish tradition emphasizes most frequently is the blessing of words. The right words speak to us where we are. They remind us that we are loved. The Jewish sages said every person should strive to say one hundred blessings a day. The origins of this practice go back to a time of illness and plague during the reign of King David. According to the sages, a hundred people were dying every day from a plague. To combat it, King David ordered that everyone say one hundred blessings a day. Soon the plague stopped. We do not have to believe this story literally to appreciate its wisdom. In times of difficulty, blessings help us cope. They remind us to look at our conditions from a different perspective. They transform us, and through us, they change the world.

MOSES'S DESPAIR

And Moses said to the LORD, "Why
have You dealt ill with Your servant,
and why have I not enjoyed Your favor,
that You have laid the burden of all
this people upon me? Did I conceive all
this people, did I bear them, that You
should say to me, 'Carry them in your
bosom as a nurse carries an infant,' to
the land that You have promised on
oath to their fathers? Where am I to get
meat to give to all this people, when they
whine before me and say, 'Give us meat
to eat!' I cannot carry all this people by
myself, for it is too much for me. If You
would deal thus with me, kill me rather,
I beg You, and let me see no more of my
wretchedness!"

Numbers 11:11-15

In Christian theology there is a concept called
"The Dark Night of the Soul." The phrase comes
from writings of St. John of the Cross, a sixteenth-
century monk, and it refers to an experience of doubt
and pain. During a dark night of the soul, we feel an
overwhelming sense of darkness, despair, and failure.
In our text, Moses seems to be experiencing a dark
night of the soul.

We can understand why. He has led the people
through the wilderness for almost forty years. They
have fought with and complained to him the whole

time. At the same time, he has defended the people to God and pleaded with God not to destroy them after the construction of the Golden Calf. In his personal life, Moses has been away from his wife and children. And to top it all off, Moses will not even get to enter the Promised Land. He will not see the realization of his journey and leadership. All of this pain and despair comes out in these words to God.

Furthermore, these words have a particular poignancy to them because Moses despairs over the same issues that have troubled him throughout the journey. It has been almost forty years, and the Israelites haven't changed much. Even after experiencing the revelation at Mount Sinai and building the portable Tabernacle, they still yearn for the "fleshpots of Egypt." They still fight with one another. They still complain about the food, and seem incapable of gratitude and faith in God's promise. So Moses feels like a failure. And he tells all of this to God.

What happens helps us understand the way God sustained Moses through the rest of the journey. It also helps us see the way God led Moses by providing exactly the response Moses needed. Then Moses leads by providing exactly the response his successor needs to hear. The whole rest of the journey is transformed by Moses's act of expressing his despair to God.

Following Moses's words, God immediately comforts him, telling Moses to gather the seventy elders of Israel to help him share the burdens of leadership. God also promises more food, and that would soon come with an abundance of quail. In these two answers,

God responds differently than previous times. God understood what Moses needed then and there. And it worked. Moses is calmer and less critical of the people.

When his successor Joshua tells Moses that two men are prophesying in the camp—a direct threat to Moses's stature as prophet and leader—Moses simply says, "Are you wrought up on my account? Would that all the LORD's people were prophets, that the LORD put His spirit upon them!" (Numbers 11:29.) Instead of feeling anger at the people, Moses expresses confidence in them. Instead of lamenting his loneliness as the sole prophet among the people, he acknowledges that God might speak to others as well. Moses seems to sense that others will help him and ultimately complete the journey of the Israelites to the Promised Land.

Aside from God's reassurance, what else in God's words changed Moses? First, Moses knew he was not alone. As the primary leader of the Israelites, Moses felt pained every time the Israelites struggled and complained. In his own despair, Moses could not be alone. God's words comforted him. The Jewish sages derived from this example a teaching that "a prisoner cannot free himself." In other words, when we feel lonely and desperate, we need others to help lift us up. We cannot do it alone. This teaching is applied throughout Jewish tradition. Consider what happens after a loved one dies in Judaism. The mourners return to their home and accept visitors for seven days. The process is called *shiva*, which means "seven." Friends, family, and acquaintances bring the mourners food, and prayer services are held at the mourners' home.

While the direct mourner—a child, a spouse, a parent—may feel like they want to be alone in their despair, the Jewish sages knew that isolation intensifies depression. We need others. As he struggled to lead the Israelites on the journey through the Promised Land, Moses struggled, and he needed God to comfort him. In our own journeys, we need each other to comfort and lift us up.

The other lesson we see in Moses's experience is that experiencing despair can transform us. It is not a condition we wish for. But neither is it a condition that permanently paralyzes us. One Jewish sage of the eighteenth century taught that "the whole world is a narrow bridge, and the most important part is not to let our fear stop us." Moses feared for the future of the Israelites. He feared their lack of faith and his own inevitable death would stop them from arriving in the Promised Land. After he shared his fear and despair with God, something changed. What changed, I believe, was his understanding of his role. Before this verse, Moses was an extraordinary leader, but he still saw completing the journey himself as part of his definition of success. He felt he was a failure that he personally did not lead the Israelites into the Promised Land. He felt he was a failure if the Israelites did not reach the same level of trust in God's word and promise as he had. But after this experience, he realizes the journey is not about him. It is about the faith and future of the Jewish people. In other words, the mission matters more than the person. And Moses trusted that with God's help, the Israelites would complete the mission.

This transformation is the reason the Torah describes Moses as "the most humble man on earth." In recognizing his limitations, Moses modeled for us what it means to be a faithful leader. In recognizing that the journey would continue without him, he recognized the difference between human finitude and divine infiniteness. This level of humility emerges when we feel a closeness to God. When Moses unburdened himself and expressed his vulnerability to God, he was not expressing a lack of faith. He was growing closer to God because the closer we grow to God, the more we recognize our humanity—our mortality—and God's transcendence. This recognition does not mean thinking less of oneself. It means thinking about oneself *less*. The journey began before us and continues after us.

In other words, humility is not about meekness. It suggests confidence in God's promise and our role in carrying it out. Our next text about the scouts Moses sends into the Promised Land illustrates this truth.

SCOUTS

Caleb hushed the people before Moses and said, "Let us by all means go up, and we shall gain possession of it, for we shall surely overcome it." But the men who had gone up with him said, "We cannot attack that people, for it is stronger than we."
Numbers 13:30-31

In Numbers 13, Moses sends twelve spies, one from each tribe of Israel, to scout out the Promised Land in preparation for the people to enter it. Ten of the spies are fearful, saying they can't conquer the people of the land, while two, Caleb and Joshua, urge trusting that God has given them the land and will bring them victory.

The story of the twelve spies prompts many questions. Why did the spies feel so afraid? Why did ten of them give negative reports, and two give very different ones? What are the lessons we can draw from it?

On the one hand, the reaction of the ten fearful spies is consistent with previous Israelite behavior. They do not trust fully in God's promise. Just as they complained about the lack of food and water and yearned for a return to Egypt, so these same Israelites lack the faith that God will ensure their victory over the Canaanites. The two who did not express fear—Caleb and Joshua—represent a small group of faith leaders. Their heroism foreshadows their significant roles later in the Bible.

The Jewish sages, however, focus much of their attention on the question of what caused the spies' fear. What did they see that caused them to recoil so strongly and doubt God's promise? This question is all the more acute because the spies were the leaders of their tribes. They knew God was with them. They had the trust of the people and, according to the sages, they knew God would not bring them to a land they could not conquer. So why the fear? They feared victory more than defeat!

They feared the change they would experience in the Promised Land.

They had grown accustomed to life in the wilderness. They felt an intense closeness to God there. They did not want to face the challenges of leading a country, building institutions, and creating an army. They were not living in "the real world." They lived in a place without real responsibility, and they had grown comfortable in it.

When they entered the Promised Land, they would have to grow up. They would have to face the challenges every nation faces. Yes, they would be doing so with God on their side. But they still felt the uncertainty. They still felt the fear. They decided they would rather stay on the journey than reach their destination.

These ten spies had a fear of success. That is a very real fear, even though we often tell ourselves we desire success. Unconsciously, we fear the hard work and risk success requires. We fear the new responsibilities and the toll they may take on our loved ones and us. We fear we might not fulfill others' expectations. The Israelites felt those same fears.

The sages also point to another element of the fear of success. They feared what they might have to do to achieve that success. Would they have to cause harm to others? Would they have to make moral compromises? Would they have to become like the Egyptians they had fled almost forty years ago? Perhaps they feared that even if they won, they would also lose.

In spite of all these legitimate fears, the sages conclude that the spies sinned. Their feelings may have been noble, but God intends for us to live in the real world of decisions, action, and moral dilemmas. We must take risks in order to grow.

We are called to create a space for God among the challenges of life, not in the isolated wilderness where manna falls from heaven, and everything is taken care of. God called Israel to live in the world as God's chosen people. Therefore, they must live in the world as it is. So what do they do? How does God ensure the journey continues and goes beyond the wilderness? Well, on the one hand, God suggests they need to reaffirm the faith they already developed. Caleb and Joshua urged this. Moses and Aaron recognize this. The people of Israel must trust God's promises, believing that God will carry them through the very real challenges they will face.

In addition to trusting in God's promise, the spies need to look more closely at themselves. According to the sages, they need to see clearly who they are. That is the message we get in one of the most poignant parts of the spies' story. They report to the people that they saw Amalekites, "We saw the Nephilim [titans] there...and we looked like grasshoppers to ourselves, and so we must have looked to them" (Numbers 13:33). They saw themselves as grasshoppers ready to get squashed by giants. But their self-assessment was completely wrong. As we learn later in the text, the Amalekites and other Canaanites feared them. As we read later in the Book of

Joshua, when the prostitute Rahab tells another set of spies, "I know that the LORD has given the country to you, because dread of you has fallen upon us, and all the inhabitants of the land are quaking before you.... We lost heart, and no man had any more spirit left because of you; for the LORD your God is the only God in heaven above and on earth below" (Joshua 2: 10-11). They assumed they knew what the Canaanites were thinking. Their assumption was based on their own self-assessment. They felt weak; thus the Canaanites must see them as weak.

By clearly illustrating the error of their ways, the Torah is teaching us to avoid this undervaluation of self and misperception of others. This is often hard to do. Think about times when you've felt self-conscious and seen other people talking. Did you imagine they might be talking about you? Did you imagine all the negative things they were saying? When I have asked this question in presentations I've given, everyone raises their hand. But most of the time we are mistaken in thinking others are talking about us. One rabbi I know quipped that most people are too busy thinking about themselves, so they don't have time to think about you. Even if we recognize this truth, how do we live by it? How do we control a fearful imagination, and thereby see ourselves more clearly?

According to the Jewish sages, the answer lies in a nearby Torah verse. It's in chapter 15 verses 39-40, "That shall be your fringe; look at it and recall all the commandments of the LORD and observe them, so that you do not follow your heart and eyes in your lustful urge. Thus you shall be reminded to observe all My commandments and to be holy to your God." *Tsitsit* are knots on the fringes of garments. Typically, they hang from a garment called a *tallit* that is worn either under one's daily garments or on top of them.

The Israelites' fears are ones many of us share.

CHAPTER 6

DEUTERONOMY

Among my most memorable experiences is spending a year studying the Book of Deuteronomy with a Christian minister. We met most weeks and reviewed different passages. The meetings started with a conversation over lunch. We talked about the power of Bible study and the various differences in Jewish and Christian interpretations. He then said, "Why don't we study the Book of Deuteronomy together?" I was a bit surprised. Why, of all books, I asked, do you want to study Deuteronomy? Because, he replied, it's the most quoted book of the Torah in the New Testament.

I had never heard that before, and I immediately agreed to study with him. I knew there was a lot we could teach each other. Deuteronomy differs significantly from the other four books of the Torah in that the plot of the story of the Jewish people does not advance much in its final book. In other words, Deuteronomy recounts what already happened in the other books of the Torah much more than it reveals new parts of the story of the Israelites' journey through the wilderness.

The recounting takes place through a series of speeches by Moses. He is both recalling Israel's journey through the wilderness and instructing the Israelites on what lessons they need to take with them into the Promised Land. He knows he will not be going with them, so he is giving them his final wisdom and instruction. Moses leaves his legacy through the lessons he imparts. We explore them in the verses below.

THE POWER OF WORDS

These are the words that Moses addressed
to all Israel on the other side of the Jordan.
Deuteronomy 1:1

Recall the time when God called out to Moses from the burning bush. God told Moses to return to Egypt, speak to the pharaoh, and lead the Israelites from slavery to the Promised Land. But Moses replied to God that he was "slow of tongue" (Exodus 4:10). In other words, he would not speak well. Some scholars suggest he may have had a lisp or some other sort of speech impediment. Whatever the case, Moses lacked confidence in himself. He felt he was not up to the task. His brother Aaron became Moses's mouthpiece, and spoke on behalf of Moses to the pharaoh.

By this point, however, more than forty years later, Moses no longer seems to have a speaking problem. Words pour forth. He has found his voice. The Hebrew name of this book—*Devarim*—means "words." God uses Moses's words to convey messages to us. And one of those messages is that words have enormous power.

Perhaps you have heard that old nursery rhyme: "Sticks and stones may break my bones, but words will never hurt me." Is that really true? Not in my experience. Words can hurt. Words can puncture. Words can wound. But words can also uplift, inspire, and bring us closer.

Words are so powerful that they can even create something out of nothing! We see this idea illustrated from the opening chapters of Torah. How does God create the universe? Through words. "God said, 'Let there be light'; and there was light" (Genesis 1:3). Creation unfolds in a pattern where God speaks, and everything comes into being. The sky, the waters, the earth literally come into existence through God's words.

The notion that words can create a new reality carries over into other parts of life. Consider, for example, a wedding ceremony. What makes a marriage? The saying of vows. The words used in vows constitute, to use the phrase of British philosopher J. L. Austin, a "performative utterance."[1] Through the uttering of these words a new, legally binding relationship is created. This understanding can help us probe even deeper into the Bible and provide a potential answer to one of our Torah portion's most ambiguous questions. In Genesis 1:26, we read God's famous words, discussed in chapter 2, "Let us make man in our image, after our likeness." While these words are sublime, they are ambiguous. What does it mean to be created in the image of God?

Many answers have been offered. For Maimonides, it was having the power of reason and intellect. Human beings operate based on thought rather than instinct, and that reflects our spark of divinity. For Saadyah Gaon, another great Jewish Bible commentator, it was having dominion over the plants and animals.[2] For other rabbis, it was having free will.[3] Some commentators point to morality and spiritual immortality as signs of the divine image within us. I prefer another answer that seems to me simpler and more accurate: human beings are created in the image of God because, like God, we create through words. While God creates the natural world through words, we create our social world through them, using language to name our surroundings and fellow human beings, to establish relationships, and to articulate the basic concepts that give our lives order. The *Targum*, the ancient translation of the Hebrew Bible into Aramaic, hints at this interpretation when it translates the words from Genesis 2:7, *vay'hi ha-adam l'nefesh chayah*, "man became a living being," as "man became a *speaking* being." Words enable us to distinguish between the past, present, and future. They allow us to describe and understand, to infuse ourselves and our world with meaning. It's easy to take our ability to use words for granted because it comes so naturally. Speaking is as easy for us as breathing, once we've learned how. Most of the time we don't consider the presence of language in our lives, the power it gives us, or the time and effort required to attain and master it.

But Moses's journey explains why the time and effort are worth it. Moses goes from one who fears answering God's call because he is slow of speech to a leader and prophet who speaks boldly to a multitude of Israelites as they plan to enter the Promised Land. Words create and sustain our world. They allow us to communicate, bond, and pass on our values and ideas to future generations, just as Moses did on the threshold of the Promised Land. The European philosopher Descartes famously said, "I think, therefore I am." In Judaism we might say, "I speak, therefore I am."

LOVE THE LORD YOUR GOD

You shall love the LORD your God with
all your heart and with all your soul and
with all your might.

Deuteronomy 6:5

In the Gospels, when someone asks Jesus to name the greatest commandment, he responds by quoting Deuteronomy 6, which is part of the Jewish prayer known as the Shema (see Matthew 22:34-40). The Shema begins with the words "Hear O Israel! The LORD is our God, the LORD alone" (Deuteronomy 6:4). It continues with our command in verse 5 to love God with all our heart, with all our soul, and with all our might.

When we first read this verse, we might think the references to heart, soul, and might are purely poetic. Perhaps they emphasize the depth of the love we should feel and display toward God. That's the way I initially understood it. But the Jewish sages believed every word of the Torah has a unique and particular meaning. God did not include words just for emphasis. Every word adds a dimension to what it means to love God.

We will examine each of these dimensions in turn, but we first need to understand the meaning of love more broadly. Generally, we think of love as a feeling. To love another person or God is to feel a deep kind of affection or devotion to them. In other words, love is primarily a noun. When we say we love someone or some being, we are saying we feel love for them.

In biblical Hebrew, however, love is primarily an action. It involves feelings, but loving someone or some being requires, by definition, certain actions that involve our heart, our words, and our hands.

According to the Jewish sages, to love God with all our heart means to study God's word. They draw this interpretation because the heart in biblical Hebrew is the seat of the mind—where our reason and intellect reside. To love God is to use our minds to study our sacred texts, which come from God. Studying them is like reading and finding meaning in a love letter. In this case, the love letter comes from God, and it is called the Old Testament. Thus, when our text says you shall love the Lord your God with all your heart, it is telling us to engage in constant study.

Furthermore, the rabbinic sages noticed a peculiar feature in the spelling of the Hebrew word for heart. In this verse, it contains an extra letter. The usual spelling is *lamed vet*. This verse, however, uses a variant spelling of *lamed vet vet*—there are two *vets*. Each ancient copy of the text scholars have uncovered has this extra letter. Some suggest this is a variant spelling that means essentially the same thing, but others see a hidden meaning in the use of this spelling. The two vets refer, they teach, to the two inclinations of the heart. They are known in Hebrew as the *yetzer hatov*, the good inclination, and the *yetzer harah*, the evil inclination. Every human being has both inclinations. Part of us yearns to do good—to perform acts of kindness—and part of us yearns to do evil—to harm and to hurt. Both inclinations will always be with us; we can't abolish the evil inclination. But we can *channel* the evil inclination and draw from its energy to do good. That is what following God's laws guides us in doing. In the case of studying God's words, using "all our heart" means applying both inclinations toward our love of God. Not only do we love God with the *yetzer hatov*, but we also take the energy of the *yetzer harah* and channel it into learning. Some rabbis even use the metaphor of the battlefield to refer to the study hall. Discussing and debating ideas is a form of warfare where we use all our aggressive energy to arrive at an understanding of what God wants of us. Using all our heart means channeling all of our inclinations when learning God's word.

The sages also offer another explanation for the double *vets*. They remind us to love God in the good times *and* the bad times. It is easy to be grateful to God and praise God's word when times are good. We may be tempted to think God is showing favor to us, and therefore we feel good spending our time studying and learning. But when times are difficult, we may feel tempted to give up on God. It is in those exact times when we can truly love God with all of our heart. It is the personal religious equivalent of the vow couples often say at a wedding, "in good times and in bad." When we commit to loving God with all of our hearts, we are promising to continue to cherish God's teachings through good times and bad.

The second part of the verse bids us to love God with all our soul. Here the sages offer several interpretations. The first seems the most obvious: to love God with all of our soul refers to prayer. Prayer ignites the soul. But then the rabbis ask the question: What is the soul? The answer is found in the Hebrew language. The word for soul—*nefesh*—also means "breath." Breath is the physical embodiment of the soul. And the soul gives us life. We can't live without breathing. Similarly, the Jewish sages taught, we can't live without a soul. Like breathing, the soul is nurtured by the body and by forces outside of the body. We can't breathe without oxygen from outside of ourselves. Similarly, the soul can't live without God. To love God with all of our soul is to let God's spirit permeate our soul through prayer. It is to give our soul over to God.

Another interpretation was offered by a modern linguistic scholar, Joel Hoffman. He contrasts the soul with the heart. In biblical Hebrew, as noted above, the heart was the seat of the intellect. The soul is the source of breath. The intellect is invisible and intangible. Breath, however, is tangible. You can feel it coming in and out of your nostrils and mouth. On a cold day, you can see your breath. According to Hoffman, our verse bids us to love God with both our tangible and intangible acts, with how we think and how we act. In other words, we love through our faith and our deeds.

We can even extend this idea of love through our faith and our works to the act of martyrdom. Martyrs show their love of God through the willingness to give up their breath, their lives, for God. In Jewish tradition, Rabbi Akiva said the words in our verses as he was burned to death by the Romans in 133 CE. A martyr loves God through giving up their breath and their soul—which are really the same—to God.

This interpretation may seem gruesome and unrealistic for a twenty-first century Christian or Jew. We don't talk often of martyrs today. But we do not need to be faced with martyrdom to appreciate the truth behind this interpretation. Love often involves a willingness to sacrifice ourselves for the object of our love. Hopefully, we never have to make that sacrifice, but a soldier who loves his or her country is often willing to die for it. Nelson Mandela withstood decades of imprisonment out of love for his people and country. Parents have died for the sake of their children. We infuse our souls into what we love, and sometimes our deepest love reflects a willingness to sacrifice ourselves for it.

The final part of our verse tells us to love our God with all our might. In three-part progressions in the Old Testament, the third part tends to be the hardest. Thus, we would expect the commandment to love God with all our might to be hardest to fulfill. But what can be harder to do than become a martyr? In other words, we have already seen the rabbinic interpretation of loving God with all our soul as reflecting a willingness to give up our lives for the sake of God's word. Can loving God with all of our might require something more difficult than that?

To answer this question, we need to understand what it means to love God with all our might. Perhaps surprisingly, the sages say loving God with all our might means with all of our financial resources. In other words, we love God with all our might by donating and supporting religious pursuits. In Hebrew, the word for such donations is *tzedakah*, which means both charity and justice. But how can donating money be harder than giving up one's life?

The Talmud addresses this question without giving a clear answer. It does so by telling a story about a man running across a field of thorny plants. The man lifts his pant legs so that they do not get scratched. But he lets the plants scratch his legs until they are bleeding profusely, and he nearly dies. After he makes it across the field and begins praying for help, he expresses gratitude for saving his pants.

Now you might be thinking no one would ever do such a thing. And perhaps the Talmud uses some exaggeration in this story. But the idea resonates: we often prioritize the wrong thing, sacrificing things of true value to preserve what is less valuable. And that lesson applies to our relationship with money. We often sacrifice parts of ourselves for money. Unlike martyrdom, which is one act, we give up important parts of ourselves frequently for the sake of money. I'm not referring to those who struggle financially or the simple truth that most people need to work to have food and shelter. Rather, think about those of us who may work an extra hour and sacrifice time we can spend with our spouse, our parents, or our children. Or think about times when we endured rain and ice to save ourselves from a ten-dollar Uber ride we could have easily covered. Now sometimes such acts can simply reflect a frugal mindset. But other times they illustrate an irrational desire to take big risks to save a little money. I once read a newspaper article about the way hotels in Las Vegas make sure their windows do not open more than a crack, so that people who lose money gambling are not tempted to jump out of the window. Indeed, for some people, money can seem more important than life itself.

Loving God with all our might, then, is about channeling energy we are capable of putting into saving money into the act of saving ourselves by studying and living God's word. It is not simply donating our money to support sacred institutions, though that itself is a critical act. It is letting our love of God flow into every act we do and every possession we own. Money plays an enormous role in society, much of it unconscious. Just think about the way we value our time and work. We assign time a value when we pay people by the hour. We even use phrases like "net worth" to describe the amount of money a person has. Money shapes our daily habits. What if we let our love of God do the same? What if we measure our actions by how much they reflected our love of God rather than the amount that we are paid or that we spent? That is the challenge presented by the commandment to love God with all of our might.

Part of the power of this verse is that it helps us see love not simply as a noun, but as a verb as well. We love God in multiple ways. Love is not just an action. It is a set of practices and commitments. Another powerful interpretation was offered by the minister friend and colleague with whom I studied Deuteronomy. He suggested that the three types of love in this verse correspond to the three aspects of the Trinity. He suggested the Father corresponds with loving God with all our might, the Son feels the love of our hearts, and the Holy Spirit is the love of our soul. In these varying interpretations, we see once again the multiple ways God speaks to us today.

GRATITUDE

Beware lest your heart grow haughty and you forget the LORD your God...and you say to yourselves, "My own power and the might of my own hand have won this wealth for me." Remember that it is the LORD your God who gives you the power to get wealth, in fulfillment of the covenant that He made on oath with your fathers, as is still the case.

Deuteronomy 8:14, 17-18

There's an old proverb about wealthy families going from shirtsleeves to shirtsleeves in three generations. The idea is that the first generation starts as workers wearing shirtsleeves, but they build a business and become wealthy. They pass on wealth to their children, who enjoy it but then spoil their own children with all the wealth they did not earn. This third generation then squanders the rest of that wealth and then goes back to manual labor and wearing shirtsleeves. The truth behind this quip is that we can become easily spoiled. When we do not have to work for something, we can easily take it for granted. And when we take something for granted, we can easily lose it.

This verse expresses God's concern that this fate may await the Israelites in the Promised Land. God has provided fully for them throughout the wilderness. God has provided manna to eat. God has provided a cloud of fire to guide them on their way. God has guided Moses in providing leadership. The Israelites are no longer slaves. God has given them all they need. And even more is coming. They are about to inherit the Promised Land, a land flowing with milk and honey. God will ensure that they conquer the tribes living there and that they build homes and settlements. God has paved the way for them.

But once they settle in and enjoy the bounty of the land, they may well start to take it for granted. They will think this bounty resulted from their efforts. They will think they conquered the land. They brought themselves out of Egypt. And they will forget God's role. They will proclaim, as our verse puts it, "My power and the might of my hand have gotten me this wealth." Once they start to think it, they will have entered into a path of decline. They will ultimately stray from God's ways and lose the Promised Land. Much of Deuteronomy is a warning to the Israelites to avoid this path. But the reality of free will means they may fall into it. Thus, Moses emphasizes again and again the imperative to acknowledge God's generosity. The positive thrust of this verse is the importance of gratitude. Gratitude will prevent the Israelites from forgetting the source of their abundance.

Gratitude, in fact, permeates much of the Torah because it is a spiritual imperative. If you look closely at the idea of gratitude, you find it makes little sense without God. Think about it. If we have no notion of God and we human beings and earth simply evolved as a result of time and random mutations, then everything we have and enjoy is ultimately a result of chance. Even if we have parents who provided for us and we feel grateful to them, the fact that we had such parents is simply a result of chance. Thus, ultimately, everything around us comes from luck. In this case, gratitude may be psychologically healthy. It can make us feel good. But it wouldn't make any spiritual sense because no one is truly responsible for giving it to us. There is no one ultimate source we can thank.

When we see the universe as God's creation, however, we know whom to thank. Prayer becomes an expression of gratitude to our Creator. The Hebrew word for Jew is *Yehudi*, which has the same root letters as the Hebrew word for gratitude, *todah*. The Jewish sages saw the core act of Judaism as giving thanks. The first prayer in the Jewish prayer book is one of gratitude, and Jewish law instructs us to say it the moment after waking up in the morning.

The Book of Deuteronomy gives us a sense of what may get in the way of that feeling of gratitude. God would not be warning the Israelites of what might happen if there wasn't a good chance it would happen. And indeed, it eventually did, leading to the conquering of the land by the Babylonians and then later, the Romans.

God warns the people against two types of entitlement. The first is one where we are spoiled by what we inherit or enjoy without any effort on our part. It is the sense of entitlement that is captured by the quip about the man born on third base who thought he'd hit a triple. In the sixth chapter of Deuteronomy, God warns about this type of entitlement, as Moses says the people will enter into "great and flourishing cities that you did not build, houses full of all good things that you did not fill, hewn cisterns that you did not hew, vineyards and olive groves that you did not plant" (6:10-11). They risk forgetting that God brought them there. They can come to think they deserve it even though they did nothing for it. Since they are on third base, they must have hit a triple.

The second type of entitlement is one where the people actually work to create wealth. They tend to their flocks, plant crops, and build houses and enjoy them. They have, indeed, hit a triple. But who taught them how to swing the bat? Who taught them the rules of the game? This second type of entitlement presents a different danger. It is not that the Israelites get spoiled. It is that they start to praise themselves rather than God.

Both types of entitlement lead us away from gratitude. Pride and arrogance become its substitute. Here is a nuance that's easy to overlook. God is not saying human beings play no role in gaining wealth or happiness. It is not a sin to acknowledge the role of our own efforts in building and creating. Each of us is born with unique talents like business acumen or critical thinking. We can use them to benefit society and ourselves. The sin is when we come to believe we are solely responsible for these talents. One of the leading rabbis of the medieval period, Nissim Gerondi, explained these distinctions by pointing to a subtle feature of the text. As he writes,

> Since your raw abilities are an endowment [rather than an achievement], you must always remember who gave it to you and where it comes from. This is why Moses says, 'Remember that it is the Lord your God who gives you the power to get wealth,' and does not say, 'Remember that it is the Lord your God who gives you wealth'…Moses says that even though it is your abilities that have earned you this wealth, remember that it is God who gave you these abilities. [4]

Our abilities may have helped create our wealth, but God gave us those abilities. Moses warns the Israelites not to forget that by remaining grateful.

The only way not to forget is to remember. That may sound circular, but remembering is much more than not forgetting. It requires active effort through ritual and learning and prayer. These acts combat ingratitude and forgetfulness. One of the critical ones is Passover, which we discussed more fully in chapter 3. But part of the observance is the recitation of a passage we find a little bit further along in Deuteronomy. It is the next and final verse of Deuteronomy that we will explore here.

> *The priest shall take the basket from your*
> *hand and set it down in front of the altar*
> *of the* LORD *your God. You shall then*
> *recite as follows before the* LORD *your*
> *God: "My father was a fugitive Aramean.*
> *He went down to Egypt with meager*
> *numbers and sojourned there; but there*
> *he became a great and very populous*
> *nation. The Egyptians dealt harshly with*
> *us and oppressed us; they imposed heavy*
> *labor upon us. We cried to the* LORD, *the*
> *God of our fathers, and the* LORD *heard*
> *our plea and saw our plight, our misery,*
> *and our oppression. The* LORD *freed us*
> *from Egypt by a mighty hand, by an*
> *outstretched arm and awesome power,*
> *and by signs and portents. He brought us*
> *to this place and gave us this land, a land*
> *flowing with milk and honey. Wherefore*
> *I now bring the first fruits of the soil*
> *which You, O* LORD, *have given me." You*

> *shall leave it before the* LORD *your God*
> *and bow low before the* LORD *your God.*
> *Deuteronomy 26:4-10*

This passage is both instructive and opaque. It helps us see the role of memory in the Bible and in spirituality. But before we unpack that, let's see what exactly this passage is about.

The setting is Jerusalem, and the time is the first harvest of the year. Right after the first fruits of the harvest appear, Israelites from across the nation were commanded by God to bring these first fruits to the Temple in Jerusalem. They would give them to a priest, watch the priest place them on the altar, and then they would recite the words of Deuteronomy 26, verses 5-10. These verses summarize the story of the birth of the Jewish people, God's redemption of them from Egypt, and their deliverance from slavery to freedom.

It is unlikely that the majority of Israelites actually carried out this practice of bringing the first fruits of the harvest to Jerusalem. It could be an arduous and impractical journey, especially if the harvest had just begun and labor was needed at their settlements. Some scholars speculate that a few people from each town would gather first fruits of their residents and then bring them to Jerusalem on behalf of the people of the town. The priests would accept the first fruits in large groups, recite the passage, keep some of the first fruits, and the rest would be shared among the people and other priests in Jerusalem.

The ritual had two critical lessons. The first is in the idea of the first fruits themselves. The first fruits were considered by the Israelites to be the best fruits. They were not to give the leftovers. They gave their best because, ultimately, God was responsible for their produce. They were honoring God by giving their best.

We might think of this in the same way we think about where we put our effort and attention in life. What do we prioritize? What do we put first? Is it our job? our hobbies? our families? our car? our church or synagogue? For the ancient Israelites, it was God.

Giving their first fruits also demonstrated trust. What if the first fruits were all that turned out well? This fear was likely a real one. By giving it as an offering, the Israelites were showing trust that God would ultimately provide. In some years, it probably felt scary. We might even think it was impractical. How could they survive if they gave all the first fruits away? This is where we learn about faith. The Israelites' willingness to sacrifice allowed God to permeate their lives. Their sacrifice opened their hearts. Faith is not certainty. It is, as Rabbi Jonathan Sacks put it, the courage to live with uncertainty. Giving the first fruits infused the Israelites with courage. We may not be farmers who grow crops today, but the sacrifices we make today can do the same for us.

These verses from Deuteronomy 26 highlight the important role of memory as well. Before we unpack this idea, however, we need to understand what exactly memory is. Memory is different from history. History is the critical study of the past. It is what is taught at most universities. In order to study the past, you look at documents and artifacts from the time. You try to gain an accurate picture of what happened. You look for causes and effects and try to link events to explain what happened and why it did so. This type of history does not seek to judge or even draw lessons from the past. It seeks simply to describe what happened.

Memory is different. Memory is about the present as much as it is about the past. It is about what we remember rather than exactly what happened. The *details* of the past matter less than the *meaning* of the past. History is what we learn at a high school or university. Memory is what we cherish in our homes and houses of worship. That is not to say the two are mutually exclusive. Memory is not the opposite of history. Rather, it serves a different role. It is like the difference between poetry and prose. They are both types of literature. But they play different roles in our hearts and minds.

This passage from Deuteronomy is about memory. It tells the story of the Jewish people in a way that speaks to their present situation as inhabitants of the land of Israel. It creates a frame for interpreting the past and present. That frame is exile and return. But the passage also has some ambiguity, which serves an important purpose.

The ambiguity comes in the opening line, "My father was a wandering Aramean." Who is the text referring to? The rabbis present two possibilities. The likeliest is that the wandering Aramean refers to Jacob. His family traced their origins to Aram, which is an area in the Middle East, and thus Jacob would be considered an Aramean by extension. And of course, it was Jacob and his sons and their descendants who went to the land of Egypt and ultimately became a nation there.

The other interpretation is that the wandering Aramean is Jacob's uncle Laban. Laban is described as an Aramean. And the rabbis come to this interpretation by reading the Hebrew text slightly differently than it is normally read. Biblical Hebrew, we recall, has no vowels or punctuation. So it is not exactly clear where commas and period should be. We have a general sense of where they go based on tradition and the meanings of the words, but there is often room for interpretation. In this case, the Jewish sages set aside the traditional reading of the service, which is "My father was a wandering Aramean," and read it as "A wandering Aramean sought to destroy my father." This reading exchanges the traditional Hebrew word *oved*, which means wander, with *ibed*, which means "destroy." They are not changing the letters in the Torah. Rather, they are altering the vowels that have traditionally been used. This type of interpretation is common. In our case, it means the wandering Aramean (Laban) tried to destroy our father (Jacob). This reading makes sense because Laban did indeed pursue Jacob after Jacob left his employ with his two daughters and much of his flock back in the book of Genesis.

This ambiguity is not simply about interpretative gymnastics. It reflects two core truths of the Jewish story. We are a wandering people. Our journey began when God called upon Abraham to leave his homeland

and journey to the Promised Land. We are also a people whom others have sought to destroy. Laban was only the first who tried. From the Egyptian pharaoh to Nazi Germany, tyrants and their followers have tried to destroy us. These verses capture that memory and truth.

What has been the secret of our survival? How have the Jewish people survived even as they have wandered and lived around the world, including thousands of years without a homeland, and been pursued by nations seeking to destroy them? Throughout history many nations and ethnic groups have disappeared. Even in the Bible itself, we see references to the Jebusites, the Hittites, and the Amorites—none of them exist anymore. Yet, the Israelites remain.

Historians might explain this by pointing to the way Jews have adapted to surrounding cultures and created new structures to maintain community when earlier structures like the Jerusalem Temple were destroyed. They may also point to distinctive Jewish practices like the dietary regulations and a unique language like Hebrew that served to tie Jews closer together and build a virtual wall between them and other populations. Think about the Amish. One of the reasons they survive is that they build a barrier between them and the larger culture. Other historians might even suggest that anti-Semitism kept the Jewish people alive because it kept us isolated as a group. Many Jewish thinkers have come to the same conclusion.

But our passage in Deuteronomy suggests a different answer. It is one not based in history, but in faith.

It gives credit not to distinctive practices or to anti-Semitism, but to God. God kept the Jewish people alive because God made a promise in the covenant. God would protect the Jewish people, and the people would remain loyal to God. Even as they strayed and stumbled at times, and even as they surely felt God was absent, God ensured the Jewish people would live. "We cried to God," we read, "and God heard our voice."

When the Israelites of the Old Testament would read this passage, they saw themselves in the text. They are the evidence that God heard the voice of their ancestors. It is their produce the text is referring to. It is their labor the text describes. They are the legacy and fulfillment of the text's vision.

And so are we. Again, while we may not be laboring in the fields and bringing produce to Jerusalem, we are the living legacy of the promises God made to Abraham. That is why the Old Testament continues to matter for Christians. Although we diverge in important ways, Jews and Christians are part of the same story. And the Old Testament remains the bridge connecting us to God and to one another.

NOTES

Chapter 1: The Torah

1   "Writing a Sefer Torah." Accessed May 12, 2021. http://
    sefertorah.net/store1/writing-a-sefer-torah?mobile=1.

2   Bruce Nolan, "Christian Gives Ruined Torah Scrolls Jewish
    Burial." Religion News Service, October 15, 2005. Accessed May
    26, 2021. https://religionnews.com/2005/10/15/christian-gives
    -ruined-torah-scrolls-jewish-burial/.

Chapter 2: Genesis

1   Rabbi Jonathan Sacks, *A Letter in the Scroll: Understanding
    Our Jewish Identity and Exploring the Legacy of the World's
    Oldest Religion* (New York: Free Press, 2004), 79.

2   William Faulkner, *Requiem for a Nun* in *Novels 1942-1954*
    (New York: Penguin Putnam, 1994), 535 (Act 1: Scene 3).

3   Benedict Carey, "Can We Get Better at Forgetting?" *New York
    Times*, March 22, 2019. Accessed May 27, 2021. https://
    www.nytimes.com/2019/03/22/health/memory-forgetting
    -psychology.html

Chapter 3: Exodus

1   Hillel Halkin, "What Ahad Ha'am Saw and Herzl Missed—and
    Vice Versa," *Mosaic*, October 5, 2016. Accessed May 27, 2021.
    https://mosaicmagazine.com/essay/history-ideas/2016/10/what
    -ahad-haam-saw-and-herzl-missed-and-vice-versa/.

2   Aaron W. Hughes, Hava Tirosh-Samuelson, eds., *Jonathan Sacks:
    Universalizing Particularity* (Netherlands: Brill, 2013), 116.

3   Abraham Joshua Heschel, *Man Is Not Alone: A Philosophy of
    Religion* (New York: Farrar, Straus & Young, Inc., 1951), 39.

4   Stanford Professor Jennifer Aaker, interview. "How to Increase
    Happiness and Meaning in Life." Accessed May 29, 2021.
    https://www.bakadesuyo.com/2013/02/happiness-aaker
    -meaning-interview/.

5   Jonah Goldberg, *Suicide of the West: How the Rebirth of
    Tribalism, Nationalism, and Socialism Is Destroying American*

Democracy (United States: Crown Publishing Group, 2020), 298.

6   Rabbi Jonathan Sacks, *The Home We Build Together: Recreating Society* (Bloomsbury Continuum, 2009), 138.

Chapter 4: Leviticus

1   Arnold Eisen, *Taking Hold of the Torah: Jewish Commitment and Community in America* (Bloomington: Indiana University Press, 2000), 74–75.

2   Arnold Eisen, *Taking Hold of the Torah*, 79.

3   Rabbi Evan Moffic, *What Every Christian Needs to Know About Judaism* (Nashville: Abingdon Press, 2020).

4   Alan Lew, *This Is Real and You Are Completely Unprepared : The Days of Awe as a Journey of Transformation* (New York: Back Bay Books, 2003).

Chapter 5: Numbers

1   Rabbi Shai Held, *The Heart of Torah: Volume 2: Essays on the Weekly Torah Portion, Volume 2, Leviticus, Numbers, and Deuteronomy* (Philadelphia: Jewish Publication Society, 2017), 103.

2   Held, *Heart of Torah*, 104.

3   Abraham Joshua Heschel, *Between God and Man: An Interpretation of Judaism* (United Kingdom: Free Press, 1997), 249.

4   Rabbi Norman Lamm, "The Election of Abraham," (sermon, The Jewish Center, New York, NY, November 2, 1968). Accessed May 30, 2021. https://archives.yu.edu/gsdl/collect/lammser m/index/assoc/HASH0161/e20c167b.dir/doc.pdf.

Chapter 6: Deuteronomy

1   J. L. Austin, *How to Do Things with Words* (Oxford: Clarendon Press, 1962), 5.

2   Quoted by Abraham Ibn Ezra in Sefer *HaYashar* on Genesis 1:26.

3   *Meshech Chochmah*, commentary on Genesis 1:26.

4   Held, *Heart of Torah*, 262.